SOUTHERN COOKING

FAMILY STYLE

SOUTHERN COOKING
FAMILY STYLE

LIANA KRISSOFF

MENUS & RECIPES FOR FAMILY GATHERINGS GRAND & SMALL

HEARST BOOKS
New York

CONTENTS

INTRODUCTION

"Southern hospitality." You hear this phrase all the time, but what does it really mean? My own time in the South has left me with some very specific feelings about these words. What it means to make people comfortable and welcome when you bring them together, what it means to be generous and open with your time and attention, what it means to feed people you care about—not only with food but with conversation and a sense of personal connection.

What I want to convey most of all in the menus in this book is the idea that entertaining in the southern style—whether you're hosting the boss for dinner or throwing a big summer barbecue with extended family or simply having an impromptu evening on the front porch with neighbors who just happen to be walking by—doesn't have to be difficult or involved, and it certainly doesn't have to be perfect. The menus that follow are meant to be used as jumping-off points, suggestions and bits of inspiration for coming up with your own meals and shaping your own celebrations in your own way. If making the cornbread for the tailgate party will stress you out, drop it from the agenda—nobody will miss the cornbread if their host is happy and having a good time. The point is that if you're flexible and easygoing, you can more fully enjoy the get-together, which means your guests will too.

The timelines included with each menu are meant to be a general plan for making dishes or parts of dishes in advance so that right before the main event you can be doing important tasks like turning off bright overhead lights and setting out candles, clearing the kitchen counters and setting up the coffee maker for later, and pouring yourself a nice stiff drink. The main goal, as I see it, is not to be exhausted when the doorbell rings. The timelines should serve as a guide to that end but can easily be molded to fit your schedule.

I have tried to select recipes that reflect the idea of seasonal eating that has long held sway in the South, particularly in rural communities, where families would grow and raise much of their own food and enjoy the best of what their land had to offer when the land was ready to offer it—hardy greens in winter and early spring, peas and asparagus in spring, a bounty of garden vegetables and fruits in summer, hard squashes and sweet potatoes and citrus (and put-up preserves) in the cold months. That said, it all depends on where you live—and what you and your friends and local farmers choose to grow. Adapt the recipes as needed, or shift menus from one season to the next if that's what works for you. Feel free to mix and match to come up with a meal that works for you and your guests. With the possible exception of Thanksgiving and Christmas dinners, which I've designed to be fairly representative of those traditional meals, these menus are by no means set in stone. They're southern in style and flavor and overall atmosphere, but there are no hard-and-fast rules, only that you and yours eat well and have a fine time doing so.

SPRING

CELEBRATING NEW BEGINNINGS

SPRING IN THE SOUTH is a long and glorious season of new beginnings, tender shoots and thinned-out baby root vegetables, welcome rain and warming sun. U-pick strawberry farms hang up "Open" placards at last, the asparagus beds awaken, the peas planted back in winter quickly get fat in their pods. If you have a CSA share, it'll likely still consist mostly of hearty greens and roots and delicate cool-season lettuces, with the occasional gemlike baby beets and fast-growing radishes and onions.

Entertaining in spring is easy for occasions such as **Derby Day**, a **Mother's Day Brunch**, or a **Porch-Sitting Evening**: Friends tend to be more than ready to get together after the doldrums of late winter, and it doesn't take much to throw a decent, uncomplicated meal together. Spring's vegetables all complement each other so well that even if you have only a little of each (say, a handful of garden peas, a colander's worth of new potatoes and baby beets, and some sweet spring onions), a colorful, special, and satisfying side dish practically makes itself in a big sauté pan. And dessert can be as simple as short-cake: biscuits (always biscuits, please) split and buttered and layered with sugar-macerated sliced strawberries and lightly sweetened whipped cream.

WHAT'S IN SEASON

Asparagus
Baby beets
Baby carrots
English and sugar snap peas
Kohlrabi
Lettuces
New potatoes
Radishes
Spring onions
Strawberries
Wild mushrooms

1

DERBY DAY

Jalapeño-Spiked Bourbon Julep

**Mango Chutney Chicken Salad
Tea Sandwiches**

Radish, Butter & Sea Salt Sandwiches

Crème Fraîche-&-Pea Deviled Eggs

Pimento Cheese Deviled Eggs

**Spicy Sausage Puffs with
Bourbon Mustard**

Sesame Crisps

Ginger beer, preferably Ale-8-One

TIMELINE

SEVERAL WEEKS IN ADVANCE	UP TO 3 DAYS IN ADVANCE	UP TO 2 DAYS IN ADVANCE	4 HOURS IN ADVANCE
• Make the Jalapeño Simple Syrup for the juleps and store in an airtight container in the refrigerator. • Chill bottles of ginger beer.	• Make the Sesame Crisps and store them in an airtight container at room temperature. • Crush ice for the juleps and keep in freezer bags in the freezer.	• Hard-cook the eggs for the deviled eggs; peel, then put in an air-tight container, cover with cold water, and store in the refrigerator. • Assemble the Spicy Sausage Puffs through step 2.	• Make the deviled eggs; arrange them on serving platters, cover with plastic, and keep in the refrigerator. • Make the bourbon mustard for the Spicy Sausage Puffs and keep at room temperature.

YOU PROBABLY DON'T NEED AN EXCUSE to throw a get-together in the heart of spring, but if you do, the running of the Kentucky Derby on the first Saturday in May is as good as any—you don't even have to watch the actual race (I've attended Derby Day parties in Louisville itself and in Athens, Georgia, and cannot recall ever seeing a horse run the race). If you're like me, you might welcome an excuse to host a fancy dress-up party, and the Derby is certainly that.

This is an early-evening soirée—the race, if you're inclined to tune in, happens a little after 6 P.M. In Louisville, of course, people start their parties first thing in the morning, and cookouts continue throughout the day during the races leading up to the big one. Think of this menu, a selection of fancy-ish nibbles, but nothing too heavy or filling, as your guests' last Derby Day stop of many.

• Make the chicken salad for the tea sandwiches and keep in the refrigerator.

• Rinse and pat dry fresh mint for the juleps; wrap in paper towels, then plastic, and keep in the refrigerator.

2 HOURS IN ADVANCE

• Assemble the Mango Chutney Chicken Salad Tea Sandwiches and Radish, Butter & Sea Salt Sandwiches, cover with plastic, and keep in the refrigerator.

• Set out sesame crisps.

LAST 30 MINUTES

• Bake the sausage puffs.

• Set out bourbon, fresh mint, Jalapeño Simple Syrup, and crushed ice for juleps, along with julep cups (preferably silver) and a muddler.

• Put ginger beer in a bucket of ice.

• Unwrap tea sandwiches and deviled eggs and garnish if desired.

• Turn on radio coverage of the Derby, or not.

JALAPEÑO-SPIKED BOURBON JULEP

INGREDIENTS

- **1** ounce Jalapeño Simple Syrup (see Note)
- **4** fresh mint leaves, plus 1 sprig for garnish
- Crushed ice
- **2½** ounces bourbon
- Club soda
- **1** very thinly sliced jalapeño round, seeded

LOUISVILLE CHEF EDWARD LEE ROUSES KENTUCKY'S CLASSIC COCKTAIL WITH A HOMEMADE JALAPEÑO SIMPLE SYRUP.

In julep cup, pour jalapeño simple syrup and add mint; gently bruise leaves with a muddler or wooden spoon. Add enough crushed ice to fill two-thirds of the cup. Add bourbon and stir gently, then add a bit more crushed ice. Top with a splash of club soda. Garnish with mint sprig and jalapeño.

NOTE: To make jalapeño simple syrup: In a small saucepan over high heat, combine 1 cup water, 1 cup sugar, and 2 roughly chopped jalapeños. Bring to a boil, stirring to dissolve sugar. Remove from heat and let steep 20 minutes. Strain syrup, discard jalapeños, and cool syrup. Simple syrup can be refrigerated, in an airtight container, up to 6 months. Makes about 1¼ cups.

EACH SERVING: About 226 calories, 0g protein, 17g carbohydrate, 0g total fat (0g saturated), 0mg cholesterol, 1mg sodium

MANGO CHUTNEY CHICKEN SALAD TEA SANDWICHES

SERVES 8 TO 10

INGREDIENTS

- ½ rotisserie chicken, meat picked and finely cubed (about 2 cups)
- ½ cup Greek-style yogurt
- ⅓ cup mango chutney, big pieces chopped
- 3 stalks celery, finely chopped (about ⅓ cup)
- 2 scallions, finely chopped
- Fresh lemon juice, to taste
- Salt, to taste
- Ground black pepper, to taste
- Butter
- 1 loaf white bread, or up to 2 loaves, as needed

THESE TEA SANDWICHES MIX MULTIPLE TEXTURES AND FLAVORS TO CREATE AN UNEXPECTEDLY SWEET AND TANGY PARTY-PERFECT BITE.

1. In a bowl, stir together the chicken, yogurt, chutney, celery, scallions, a squeeze lemon juice, salt, and pepper. Taste and adjust seasonings, if necessary.

2. Butter one side of each slice of bread. Divide salad among half of the slices of bread; top with remaining buttered slices. Take desired cookie cutter shape and cut out the sandwiches (it may help to use a knife to trim around the cookie cutter for a cleaner cut).

EACH SERVING: About 282 calories, 11g protein, 34g carbohydrate, 13g total fat (6g saturated), 31mg cholesterol, 580mg sodium

GET FANCY

IT MAY AT FIRST SEEM A LITTLE RIDICULOUS, sure, but if you're going to dress formally for a party in the South, early May is a fine time to do it. Take a gander at the dress codes and "apparel recommendations" on the official Kentucky Derby website if you need inspiration (or fun wording for those engraved invitations). Think: seersucker in traditional blue or more interesting olive or gray, straw fedoras or boaters, long muslin skirts, pastel flounces, and—of course—the most outrageous women's hats you can come up with. If your hat is too sedate straight out of the box, gather a bunch of random decorations—silk butterflies and flowers, feathered-bird Christmas ornaments, magnolia cones and branches of the tree's big waxy leaves, strings of lace and fluffs of tulle—and go to work with the glue gun or needle and thread, building the arrangement as high and wide as possible.

RADISH, BUTTER & SEA SALT SANDWICHES

INGREDIENTS

- 1 loaf pumpernickel bread, or up to 2 loaves, as needed
- Butter
- 1 bunch radishes, thinly sliced
- Sea salt

THESE TEA SANDWICHES HAVE A BIT OF BITE—THEY'RE INSPIRED BY THE CLASSIC FRENCH NIBBLE OF RAW RADISHES DIPPED IN SWEET BUTTER.

Spread one side of each slice of bread with butter (this will keep your tea sandwiches from drying out too much). Layer half of bread slices with radishes. Sprinkle radish layer with sea salt. Place remaining buttered slices on top of salted radishes, forming a sandwich. Take desired cookie cutter shape and cut out the sandwiches (it may help to use a knife to trim around the cookie cutter for a cleaner cut).

EACH SERVING: About 173 calories, 5g protein, 24g carbohydrate, 7g total fat (4g saturated), 14mg cholesterol, 620mg sodium

CRÈME FRAÎCHE-&-PEA DEVILED EGGS

INGREDIENTS

12 large eggs
2 teaspoons white vinegar
⅔ cup petite peas, blanched
½ cup crème fraîche
¼ cup olive oil
  Salt, to taste
  Freshly ground pepper, to taste

A SPRING PEA PUREE AND LIGHT AND CREAMY CRÈME FRAÎCHE ADD A FRESH BURST OF FLAVOR TO THIS PICNIC FAVORITE.

1. In a large pot over high heat, bring eggs, vinegar, and enough cold water to cover by 1 inch to a boil. Reduce heat to medium-high to maintain a medium boil and cook eggs for 8 minutes. Drain and run eggs under cool water. Fill a bowl with cold water, add eggs, and let sit for 20 minutes to cool at room temperature.

2. Peel eggs and halve lengthwise. Remove yolks and transfer to a medium bowl. Set aside whites on a serving plate. With a fork, break up yolks until fluffy.

3. In a food processor, puree peas, crème fraîche, olive oil, salt, and freshly ground pepper.

4. To yolks, add pea mixture and stir to combine. Fill egg whites. Cover and refrigerate at least 30 minutes, or until ready to serve.

EACH SERVING: About 80 calories, 4g protein, 1g carbohydrate, 7g total fat (2g saturated), 100mg cholesterol, 33mg sodium

TIP To center yolks to create indentations in egg whites that will be easier to fill, turn the egg carton upside down in the refrigerator two to three hours before cooking the eggs.

PIMENTO CHEESE DEVILED EGGS

INGREDIENTS

12 large eggs

2 teaspoons white vinegar

2 ounces Cheddar cheese, grated (about ½ cup)

3 ounces (6 tablespoons) cream cheese

¼ cup mayonnaise

3 tablespoons diced pimentos

½ teaspoon dry mustard

Salt, to taste

Freshly ground pepper, to taste

A NEW TAKE ON A SOUTHERN PARTY FOOD CLASSIC, THESE DEVILED EGGS ARE FLAVORED WITH A CREAMY PIMENTO CHEESE MIXTURE.

1. In a large pot over high heat, bring eggs, vinegar, and enough cold water to cover by 1 inch to a boil. Reduce heat to medium-high to maintain a medium boil and cook eggs for 8 minutes. Drain and run eggs under cool water. Fill a bowl with cold water, add eggs, and let sit for 20 minutes to cool at room temperature.

2. Peel eggs and halve lengthwise. Remove yolks and transfer to a medium bowl. Set aside whites on a serving plate. With a fork, break up yolks until fluffy.

3. To yolks, add Cheddar cheese, cream cheese, mayonnaise, diced pimentos, dry mustard, salt, and freshly ground pepper; mix. Fill egg whites. Cover and refrigerate for at least 30 minutes, or until ready to serve.

EACH SERVING: About 78 calories, 4g protein, 0.5g carbohydrate, 7g total fat (2g saturated), 100mg cholesterol, 74mg sodium

SPICY SAUSAGE PUFFS WITH BOURBON MUSTARD

INGREDIENTS

- 1 package (14-ounce) all-butter puff pastry, thawed
  Flour, for dusting
- 8 hot-dog-size, fully-cooked smoked andouille chicken sausages, ends trimmed off
- 1 large egg, lightly beaten with 1 teaspoon water

BOURBON MUSTARD

- 2 tablespoons bourbon
- ⅓ cup Creole or grainy Dijon mustard
- 1 tablespoon honey

THESE ARE LIKE PIGS IN A BLANKET FOR GROWN-UPS: SPICY CHICKEN SAUSAGES ARE WRAPPED IN BUTTERY PUFF PASTRY, THEN BAKED AND SERVED WITH A TANGY, BOURBON-SPIKED MUSTARD SAUCE.

1. Unfold pastry, lightly dust both sides with flour, and place on a floured surface. Using a pizza wheel, cut pastry crosswise into 16 (½-inch-wide) strips. Start spiraling a pastry strip around a sausage, without overlapping the pastry. When you come to the end of the first strip, start a second (press ends together) and continue wrapping until sausage is covered. Wrap remaining sausages.

2. Evenly space sausages on parchment-lined baking sheet. Refrigerate 1 hour (or up to 2 days, covered) before baking.

3. Preheat oven to 375°F. Brush pastries with egg mixture. Bake until puffed and golden, 22 to 25 minutes. Cool 5 minutes. Using a serrated knife, cut each pastry into thirds and skewer with a toothpick. Serve with bourbon mustard for dipping.

4. Prepare bourbon mustard: Heat bourbon in a small saucepan over medium heat until warm. Carefully ignite it. When the alcohol is burned off (i.e., the flame goes out), pour into a small bowl. Stir in mustard and honey. (Can be made several hours ahead and kept at room temperature.)

EACH SERVING: About 131 calories, 6g protein, 8g carbohydrate, 8g total fat (4g saturated), 44mg cholesterol, 328mg sodium

SESAME CRISPS

INGREDIENTS

Nonstick cooking spray

6 tablespoons (¾ stick) butter, softened

⅔ cup sugar

1 teaspoon vanilla extract

¼ teaspoon salt

¼ teaspoon baking powder

1 large egg

½ cup plus 2 tablespoons all-purpose flour

8 teaspoons white sesame seeds, toasted

THESE ARE SIMILAR TO THE THIN, CRISP COOKIES KNOWN AS BENNE WAFERS (BENNE SEEDS ARE SESAME SEEDS) THAT ARE POPULAR THROUGHOUT THE SOUTH BUT ESPECIALLY IN CHARLESTON, SOUTH CAROLINA. THEY'RE DELICATE AND REFINED, PERFECT LITTLE SWEETS FOR A FANCY-DRESS DERBY DAY EVENT.

1. Preheat oven to 350°F. Spray two large cookie sheets with nonstick cooking spray.

2. In large bowl, with mixer on medium speed, beat butter, sugar, vanilla, salt, and baking powder until blended. Add egg; beat until well combined. With spoon, stir in flour.

3. Spoon half the dough into a small bowl; stir in toasted white sesame seeds. Stir black sesame seeds into dough remaining in large bowl.

4. Drop doughs by rounded teaspoons, about 3 inches apart, onto cookie sheets. Place cookie sheets on two oven racks. Bake cookies about 8 minutes, rotating cookie sheets between upper and lower racks halfway through baking time, until cookies are just set and edges are golden. Let cookies remain on cookie sheets about 30 seconds to set further before removing to racks to cool.

5. Wipe cookie sheets clean with paper towels; spray again with nonstick cooking spray. Repeat step 4 with remaining cookie doughs. Store cookies in tightly covered container.

NOTE: **You can substitute black sesame seeds (available at Asian grocers) for up to half the white sesame seeds, if you like.**

EACH SERVING: About 45 calories, 1g protein, 6g carbohydrate, 2g total fat (1g saturated), 11mg cholesterol, 40mg sodium

2
MOTHER'S DAY BRUNCH

Country Ham & Cheddar Grits Soufflé

Buttermilk Biscuits

Sweet Potato Waffles

Peach Preserves

Maple-Glazed Bacon

Banana Cake with Coconut-Pecan Crumb Topping

White Iced Tea

Simple green salad

TIMELINE

PREVIOUS SUMMER

• Make the Peach Preserves. (or purchase good-quality jam).

SEVERAL DAYS IN ADVANCE

• Make salad dressing: minced shallot, a bit of grainy mustard, 1 part vinegar, 3 parts oil, salt, and pepper; refrigerate.

UP TO 1 DAY IN ADVANCE

• Make Banana Cake with Coconut-Pecan Crumb Topping.

• Make White Iced Tea.

• Rinse and spin-dry greens for salad. Wrap in paper towels, then tuck into a plastic bag and refrigerate.

• Prepare Maple-Glazed Bacon through step 1 and refrigerate.

THE NIGHT BEFORE

• Prepare ingredients for Country Ham and Cheddar Grits Soufflé: grease and refrigerate baking dish, dice ham, chop onion, mince garlic and put in covered bowl in fridge, separate eggs, combine grated cheddar and chopped parsley.

• In separate bowls, prepare dry and wet ingredients for Sweet Potato Waffles (step 1). Cover bowl of wet ingredients and refrigerate.

T HE SECOND SUNDAY IN MAY IS MOTHER'S DAY (mark your calendar and don't forget it), and it happens to be prime time for the most fragrant and beautiful spring flowers. Think of this lovely, simple brunch as a showcase for your flower-arranging skills as much as your prowess in the kitchen: pick armfuls of daffodils, tulips, fruit blossoms, if you can spare them, and lily-of-the-valley and lilacs if you live up north. And while you're outside, gather plenty of fresh herbs for the iced tea and to toss into a green salad to serve alongside the country ham soufflé.

Whether you're a sweet-breakfast or savory-breakfast type, there's something in this brunch menu for you—and arguably the Maple-Glazed Bacon will appeal to both camps. I'm including a recipe for refrigerator peach preserves here even though peaches won't be in season for months yet—it's just so southern with biscuits (or with the waffles); of course you can use store bought peach or berry jam, or your own if you had the foresight to put up some jars last summer.

UP TO 2 HOURS IN ADVANCE

• Make Buttermilk Biscuits.

• Glaze bacon and set aside at room temperature.

1 HOUR IN ADVANCE

• Make soufflé and put in the oven 45 minutes before serving time. Turn off oven

• Arrange flowers, set table.

so it can be used last-minute to keep waffles warm.

• Finish waffle batter (pour wet into dry, then stir in melted butter).

• Pull vinaigrette from refrigerator and whisk or shake to recombine as it comes to room temperature.

• Pull good butter from refrigerator to soften for easy spreading on waffles and biscuits.

LAST MINUTE

• Make a fresh pot of coffee.

• Cook waffles.

COUNTRY HAM & CHEDDAR GRITS SOUFFLÉ

INGREDIENTS

- 4 tablespoons (½ stick) unsalted butter
- 1½ tablespoons plain dried breadcrumbs
- 1½ tablespoons grated Parmesan cheese (mix with breadcrumbs)
- 1 can (14½ ounces) chicken broth
- 1 cup light cream or half-and-half
- ¼ teaspoon salt
- ¾ cup quick-cooking grits (not instant)
- ½ cup chopped onion
- 1 clove garlic, minced
- ¾ cup finely diced smoked ham
- 1 teaspoon hot red pepper sauce
- 6 large eggs, separated
- 1½ cups shredded sharp Cheddar cheese
- 3 tablespoons fresh chopped parsley

GRITS AND COUNTRY HAM CONTRIBUTE DOWN-HOME FLAVORS, BUT THIS GOLDEN BAKED DISH LOOKS QUITE SOPHISTICATED ON THE BRUNCH TABLE.

1. Preheat oven to 375°F. With 2 tablespoons of the butter, grease shallow 2½- to 3-quart baking dish or a 13" by 9" by 2" baking dish; coat dish with breadcrumb and Parmesan mixture, turning dish to evenly distribute. Refrigerate dish while making soufflé mixture.

2. In medium saucepan, bring broth, cream, and salt to a boil; slowly stir in grits. Reduce heat to low, cover, and cook 5 minutes, or until creamy and thick.

3. Meanwhile, in small skillet, melt remaining 2 tablespoons butter over medium heat. Add onion and garlic; cook 3 minutes, or until translucent. Add ham; cook 1 minute. Remove from heat. When grits are cooked, stir in onion mixture and hot pepper sauce. Stir in egg yolks, one at a time, until blended. Stir in Cheddar and parsley, until cheese is melted and mixture is smooth.

4. Beat egg whites with an electric mixer until stiff. Stir one-quarter of the whites into grits mixture to lighten; fold in remaining whites. Spoon the soufflé mixture into chilled baking dish. Bake 40 to 45 minutes, until puffed and golden. Serve immediately.

EACH SERVING: About 458 calories, 21g protein, 22g carbohydrate, 32g total fat (18g saturated), 273mg cholesterol, 1,026mg sodium

COUNTRY HAM

WHAT'S THE DIFFERENCE BETWEEN COUNTRY HAM AND CITY HAM? Country ham is salted and hung to cure for up to several months, (usually) smoked, then aged for as long as several years. A good country ham is similar in saltiness and funkiness to Italian prosciutto, but is drier and usually served cooked, if only lightly. City hams are wet-brined and then (usually) smoked; they have a mild, almost sweet ham flavor compared to stronger and more

assertive country ham, and are moister. You can use either variety in this soufflé, but if you can find it country ham will be more authentically southern. And while you're in a grocery store that carries country ham, pick up some White Lily (soft winter wheat) flour for your biscuits.

BUTTERMILK BISCUITS

INGREDIENTS

- 2 cups self-rising flour, plus at least 1 cup more for dusting work surface
- 4 tablespoon (½ stick) butter, at room temperature, cut into small pieces, plus 1 tablespoon melted
- ¼ cup cream cheese, at room temperature
- ¾ cup buttermilk

CREAM CHEESE IS THE SURPRISE INGREDIENT IN THESE BITE-SIZE DELIGHTS BY CARRIE MOREY OF CALLIE'S BISCUITS AND SOUTHERN TRADITIONS.

1. Set a rack in the middle of oven and preheat to 500°F. Meanwhile, in large bowl, combine 2 cups of the flour, butter pieces, and cream cheese, using your fingers to cut in the butter and cream cheese until the mixture resembles cottage cheese.

2. Make a well in the center of the mixture. Add buttermilk and mix with your hands or a small rubber spatula.

3. Sprinkle flour over the dough. Run a rubber spatula between the bowl and the dough, then sprinkle the exposed dough with more flour.

4. Turn dough out onto a well-floured surface. Generously sprinkle dough and rolling pin with flour. Roll out to a ½-inch-thick oval. (Do not knead.)

5. Pour about ½ cup flour into small bowl. Dip 2-inch square metal biscuit cutter into the flour; then cut out biscuits, dipping cutter back into the flour as necessary. (As long as the dough remains wet on the inside, you can use as much flour on the outside as needed to handle it.) Gather excess dough, roll it out to a ½-inch-thick oval, and continue cutting biscuits as above. Place biscuits, sides touching, in a cast-iron skillet or baking pan lined with parchment. Brush the tops of the biscuits with melted butter.

6. Place pan in oven and immediately reduce temperature to 450°F. Bake biscuits until tops are golden, 16 to 18 minutes, rotating halfway through cooking time.

EACH SERVING: About 268 calories, 6g protein, 37g carbohydrate, 10g total fat (5g saturated), 28mg cholesterol, 49mg sodium

SWEET POTATO WAFFLES

⌐| MAKES 8

INGREDIENTS

½ cups all-purpose flour

⅓ cup sugar

1 tablespoon baking powder

2 teaspoons ground ginger

½ teaspoon baking soda

½ teaspoon salt

¼ teaspoon allspice

1½ cups milk

1 cup mashed leftover cooked sweet potatoes

4 large eggs

¾ teaspoon vanilla extract

4 tablespoons (½ stick) unsalted butter, melted, plus more for brushing waffle iron and pats for serving

Maple syrup, for serving

LINDA OWENS SURFUS, THE *COUNTRY LIVING* MAGAZINE READER WHO CREATED THIS RECIPE, RECOMMENDS GRATING ORANGE ZEST INTO THE BATTER FOR EXTRA FLAVOR.

1. Preheat oven to 200°F. In large mixing bowl, combine flour, sugar, baking powder, ginger, baking soda, salt, and allspice. In medium bowl, whisk together milk, sweet potatoes, eggs, and vanilla until combined.

2. Stir sweet potato mixture into flour mixture until combined. Stir in melted butter until just blended—some lumps will remain.

3. Place wire rack on baking pan and set in oven. Heat waffle iron to medium-high and lightly brush grids with melted butter. Ladle about ½ cup batter into center of iron (grids should be full but not overflowing), close, and cook until iron stops steaming and waffles are golden brown, about 4 minutes (or make according to your manufacturer's instructions). Transfer waffles to wire rack in oven to keep warm. Repeat with remaining batter. Serve with pats of butter and maple syrup.

EACH SERVING: About 323 calories, 9g protein, 49g carbohydrate, 10g total fat (6g saturated), 113mg cholesterol, 693mg sodium

PEACH PRESERVES

INGREDIENTS

3½ cups sugar

2 pounds fresh peaches (about 5); pitted, peeled, and quartered

Juice of ½ lemon

THIS RECIPE COMES FROM CHEF AND AUTHOR NORMA JEAN DARDEN. TO SEE MORE OF NORMA JEAN'S RECIPES, CHECK OUT HER CLASSIC COOKBOOK, *SPOONBREAD AND STRAWBERRY WINE*, A WONDERFUL COLLECTION OF SOUTHERN HERITAGE RECIPES AND FAMILY HISTORY.

1. Bring sugar and 2 cups water to a boil in large saucepan. Add peaches and cook over medium heat until syrup is clear and slightly thickened and peaches are tender, 8 to 10 minutes. Cover, refrigerate, and let stand overnight.

2. Remove fruit from syrup and transfer to pint jars. Place remaining syrup and the lemon juice in medium saucepan and bring to a boil, stirring frequently, until syrup reaches the consistency of molasses or honey. Pour syrup over peaches and let cool to room temperature. Cover and keep refrigerated up to 3 weeks.

EACH SERVING: About 191 calories, .5g protein, 49g carbohydrate, 0g total fat (0g saturated), 0mg cholesterol, 0mg sodium

MAPLE-GLAZED BACON

INGREDIENTS

- 12 slices bacon
- ¼ cup pure maple syrup
- 1 teaspoon Dijon mustard
- 1 teaspoon brown sugar

1. Cook bacon: In large skillet over medium-high heat, cook bacon in batches until it is browned but not crisp. Drain on paper towels and set aside.

2. Glaze bacon: Combine maple syrup, mustard, and brown sugar in small bowl and set aside. Return bacon to skillet, brush with the glaze, and turn. Cook glazed side down 2 minutes over low heat. Glaze, turn, and cook an additional 2 minutes over low heat. Repeat until all of the glaze is used; serve immediately.

EACH SERVING (3 SLICES): About 166 calories, 6g protein, 14g carbohydrate, 10g total fat (3g saturated), 16mg cholesterol, 337mg sodium

BANANA CAKE WITH COCONUT-PECAN CRUMB TOPPING

⊰| MAKES ONE 9-INCH ROUND CAKE (12 SERVINGS)

INGREDIENTS

COCONUT-PECAN TOPPING

1/2 cup pecans, toasted and chopped

1/4 cup unsweetened shredded coconut, toasted

1/4 cup all-purpose flour

1/4 cup packed dark brown sugar

1/4 teaspoon ground cinnamon

2 tablespoons butter or margarine

BANANA CAKE

11/2 cups all-purpose flour

1 teaspoon baking powder

1/2 teaspoon baking soda

1/4 teaspoon salt

1/8 teaspoon ground cinnamon

4 tablespoons butter or margarine, at room temperature

1/2 cup packed dark brown sugar

3 tablespoons pure honey

2 large eggs, lightly beaten

1 cup mashed very ripe bananas (about 3 medium)

1 teaspoon vanilla extract

FOR BEST FLAVOR, MAKE SURE TO USE VERY RIPE BANANAS WHEN MAKING THIS IRRESISTIBLE BANANA CAKE. THE PEELS SHOULD BE COVERED WITH BLACK SPOTS.

1. Prepare coconut-pecan topping: In medium bowl, combine pecans, coconut, flour, brown sugar, and cinnamon. With pastry blender or two knives used scissor-fashion, cut in butter until mixture resembles coarse crumbs, with a few pea-size chunks remaining.

2. Prepare banana cake: Preheat oven to 350°F. Grease 9-inch spring-form pan; line bottom with parchment and grease parchment. On sheet of waxed paper, mix flour, baking powder, baking soda, salt, and cinnamon until well blended. In large bowl, with mixer on medium speed, beat butter, brown sugar, and honey until light and creamy, about 5 minutes, scraping bowl occasionally. Gradually add eggs, one at a time, beating after each addition. On low speed, add half of flour mixture, then mashed bananas, and vanilla. Add remaining flour mixture and beat just until smooth.

3. Spoon batter into prepared pan and spread evenly. Sprinkle with crumb topping. Bake 50 to 55 minutes or until toothpick inserted in center cake comes out clean. Cool in pan on wire rack 10 minutes. With small metal spatula, loosen cake from side of pan and remove. Cool completely. (Cake can be wrapped tightly in plastic and kept at room temperature up to 1 day.)

EACH SERVING: About 255 calories, 4g protein, 37g carbohydrate, 11g total fat (5g saturated), 51mg cholesterol, 205mg sodium

WHITE ICED TEA

INGREDIENTS

4 white tea bags

4 cups boiling water

½ cup sugar

Fresh tarragon sprigs (or other fresh herbs), to taste

USE FRESH TARRAGON OR CREATE YOUR OWN SIGNATURE ICED TEA BY TRYING THIS RECIPE WITH OTHER FRESH HERBS, SUCH AS ROSEMARY, LAVENDER, OR MINT. MAKE THIS ONLY A FEW HOURS BEFORE SERVING TO KEEP FLAVORS CRISP AND DISTINCT.

1. Steep tea bags in boiling water, then remove bags and chill tea.

2. Bring 1 cup water and the sugar to a boil, add tarragon, and remove from heat; steep until cool. Sweeten chilled tea to taste with the tarragon syrup, which will add a licorice note to the tea.

EACH SERVING: About 98 calories, 0g protein, 25g carbohydrate, 0g total fat (0g saturated), 0mg cholesterol, 0.25mg sodium

SWEET TEA

WHEN MY FAMILY MOVED TO RURAL GEORGIA when I was a kid, our neighbor, Teresa, was our primary source of information about southern foodways. My mom was shocked the first time she saw her make a pitcher of iced tea. Teresa put two heaping cups of sugar in the pitcher—so much that we wondered if it would crystallize into rock candy if left out for a couple weeks with a string in it. There's no need to make tea so insanely sweet (in fact, please don't); just a touch of sugar is plenty as long as it's dissolved in the hot tea before it's chilled. You'll have to experiment a bit to find the right number of tea bags (Luzianne brand is favored by most southerners I know) and steeping time for your taste. If cloudiness bothers you, lift the tea bags from the tea without squeezing them, and let the hot tea cool to room temperature gradually before adding ice and cold water and refrigerating it.

3

PORCH-SITTING EVENING

Cheese Straws

Spicy Cocktail Pecans

Garden Herb Spritzer

**Fresh berries & sugar-snap peas,
or any other spring
garden goodies to serve raw**

Craft beers

TIMELINE

UP TO 1 WEEK IN ADVANCE

• Make Spicy Cocktail Pecans; let cool, then store in airtight container at room temperature.

UP TO 2 DAYS IN ADVANCE

• Make Cheese Straws; let cool, then store in airtight container at room temperature.

BEFORE IT GETS TOO HOT TO DO ANYTHING but sit in front of a fan while misting yourself with a water bottle, take advantage of the cooler evenings and have some friends over for some old-fashioned porch sitting. There's something about a porch at dusk that encourages good conversation (white wine spritzers and tasty snacks like Cheese Straws and Spicy Cocktail Pecans might also play a role). Plus it's easy to invite neighborhood folks to join you if they happen to be walking by. If you don't have a porch, a stoop will do, as will a carport or just a few chairs in the yard.

My preparation timeline begins a week in advance, but please don't hesitate to throw an evening together at the spur of the moment, and toss this menu right out the window. Mix some drinks, arrange a platter of nibbles (got hummus and some nuts? You're halfway there!), and don't sweat the details.

1 DAY IN ADVANCE

• Make Garden Herb Spritzer through step 3 and put in freezer to become slushy.

• Chill tonic water and beer. Chill glasses for spritzers, if there's room in the fridge or freezer.

• Rinse fresh herb sprigs, pat dry, wrap in paper towel, and stash in a plastic bag in the refrigerator to use for garnish for spritzer.

• String lights on porch.

LAST 30 MINUTES

• Sweep porch and dust chairs and surfaces.

• Rinse fresh fruit and sugar-snap peas and set out in bowls for raw snacking.

• Put beer in an ice bucket for serving.

CHEESE STRAWS

INGREDIENTS

- 3 (10-ounce) bricks of sharp Cheddar cheese, at room temperature
- 1 cup (2 sticks) butter, softened
- 4 cups sifted all-purpose flour
- 2 teaspoons salt
- ⅛ teaspoon ground black pepper
- ⅛ teaspoon cayenne (ground red pepper)
- 1 dash garlic powder

THIS RECIPE FOR THE CLASSIC SOUTHERN SNACK IS FROM *GEORGIA COOKING IN AN OKLAHOMA KITCHEN: RECIPES FROM MY FAMILY TO YOURS* **BY TRISHA YEARWOOD.**

1. Preheat oven to 325°F.

2. Put cheese and butter in bowl of heavy-duty electric mixer. Using heaviest mixer attachment, beat until mixture has consistency of whipped cream, about 30 minutes.

3. On a sheet of waxed paper, sift 3 cups of the flour with the salt, black pepper, cayenne pepper, and garlic powder. Gradually add the seasoned flour to the cheese mixture by large spoonfuls, beating well after each addition. Add the remaining 1 cup unseasoned flour until the dough is somewhat stiff but still soft enough to be pushed though a cookie press; you may not need to add all the flour.

4. Lightly spray a cookie sheet with nonstick cooking spray. Put a portion of the dough into a cookie press fitted with the star tube and press the dough onto cookie sheet in long strips. Bake 20 minutes. The cheese straws should be golden brown and crisp.

5. With a sharp knife, cut the long strips into 3-inch lengths. Use a flat, thin spatula to remove the cheese strips from pan. Allow them to cool on a wire rack. When they are completely cool, store in airtight container.

EACH SERVING: About 137 calories, 5g protein, 8g carbohydrate, 10g total fat (6g saturated), 29mg cholesterol, 241mg sodium

SPICY COCKTAIL PECANS

INGREDIENTS

- ½ cup (1 stick) unsalted butter, melted
- 4 teaspoons Tabasco sauce
- 2 teaspoons Worcestershire sauce
- 2 teaspoons sea salt
- 1 teaspoon garlic powder
- 6 cups pecan halves (about 1½ pounds)

THIS IS ONE FIRECRACKER OF A SNACK. THE HEALTHY NUT FATS WILL BALANCE THE DRINKS, AND THE TABASCO WILL KEEP THE CONVERSATION LIVELY.

1. Preheat oven to 325°F with racks set in the top and middle positions. Meanwhile, in small bowl, stir together all ingredients except pecans.

2. Place pecans in large bowl. Pour butter mixture over pecans, tossing to combine. Spread pecans evenly on two baking sheets and bake until toasted and fragrant, 12 to 15 minutes, rotating pans halfway through. Transfer to paper towel–lined baking pan and let cool completely, 20 minutes.

EACH SERVING (¼ CUP): About 206 calories, 2g protein, 4g carbohydrate, 22g total fat (4g saturated), 10mg cholesterol, 170mg sodium

EMBRACE THE DUSK ⟩

ONE OF THE FIRST THINGS I NOTICED when I moved back to the South after a fair number of years in the Northeast is that people tend to over-light their parties. (My New Yorker husband has been known to go through a party venue turning off overhead lights, and it's not for nothing that parties invariably get better after he arrives.) On a porch at nighttime, it's hard to mess up the lighting situation. Light a couple of candles or plug in a string of lanterns or a strand of tiny electric lights (funky multicolored or elegant clear ones depending on your style), and that's it; leave the glaring porch lights off. Talk is better when the lights are low, and this kind of gathering is all about encouraging conversation.

GARDEN HERB SPRITZER

INGREDIENTS

- 1 **bottle (750ml) white wine, such as Chardonnay**
- **Juice and grated zest of 5 large lemons (about 1 cup juice and 5 tablespoons zest), plus more if desired**
- 1 **cup sugar, plus more if desired**
- 2 **bunches lemon thyme or fresh herb of choice**
- **Ice**
- 1½ **liters tonic water**

1. In large pot, bring wine, lemon juice, 1 cup water, and sugar to a boil. Add lemon zest. Reduce heat to medium-low and simmer 5 minutes.

2. Remove pot from heat, add 1 bunch thyme, and let steep 15 minutes. While mixture is still hot, add a few more thyme sprigs, plus more sugar and lemon juice, if desired.

3. Set 1½-quart container in a bowl and fill bowl halfway with ice. Strain wine mixture into container. Place bowl in freezer and add water to cover ice. Chill until cold and mixture is slushy, about 8 hours.

4. Divide among glasses, then top off with tonic water. Add ice, if desired. Garnish with thyme sprigs.

EACH SERVING: About 181 calories, 0g protein, 30g carbohydrate, 0g total fat, 0mg cholesterol, 5mg sodium

SUMMER

TAKING IT OUTSIDE

SCOUT'S FAMOUS DESCRIPTION of the hot season in Harper Lee's southern classic *To Kill a Mockingbird* is not far off the mark: "Men's stiff collars wilted by nine in the morning. Ladies bathed before noon, after their three-o'clock naps, and by nightfall were like soft teacakes with frostings of sweat and sweet talcum" (though these days most folks aren't able to indulge in midafternoon naps). Summer in the modern South is a study in extremes: There are no qualms about hosting bang-up cookouts and family picnics in the heat of the day (shade trees, minimal physical activity, and water are key for a **Family Reunion BBQ** or a **Father's Day Backyard Campout**), perhaps because you can count on there being a cool space somewhere close by—home, a dark bar, a megachurch—any of these will do.

The menus that follow are pretty much meant to be enjoyed outdoors. Turn on a hose for a **Sprinkler Party** if water's not scarce. When night approaches, keep it simple and enjoy the view with a **Coastal Dinner Party**. And always consider adopting the simple but effective lemonade cure detailed in Lee's novel: "Lemonade in the middle of the morning was a summertime ritual. Calpurnia set a pitcher and three glasses on the porch, then went about her business."

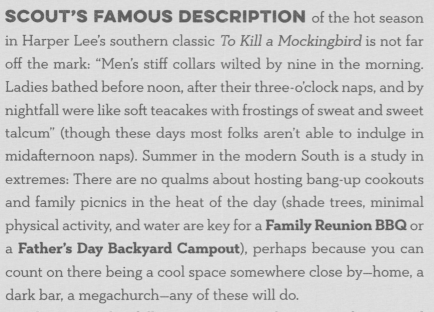

WHAT'S IN
SEASON

Blackberries
Blueberries
Field peas
Figs
Green beans
Herbs
Melons
Okra
Peaches & nectarines
Peppers
Sweet corn
Tomatoes
Zucchini & yellow squash

FAMILY REUNION BBQ

BBQ Chicken Thighs

Collards with Pickled
Red Onions

Green Beans with Toasted
Benne Seeds

Sweet Potato Salad with
Lemony Buttermilk Dressing

Cabbage-&-Cilantro
Slaw

Baked Macaroni

Jumbo Pecan-Date
Oatmeal Cookies

Nectarine & Blueberry
Cobbler

Watermelon Limeade

Burgers

Beer

TIMELINE

UP TO 1 WEEK IN ADVANCE

• Make Jumbo Pecan-Date Oatmeal Cookies; store in an airtight container at room temperature.

UP TO 2 DAYS IN ADVANCE

• Make pickled onions (through step 2 of Collards with Pickled Red Onions) and refrigerate.

• Clean and chop collard greens and refrigerate.

1 DAY IN ADVANCE

• Prepare BBQ Chicken Thighs through step 2: rub thighs and refrigerate; make sauce and refrigerate; separately.

• Make Green Beans with Toasted Benne Seeds (reserving sesame seeds for sprinkling on the salad at the last minute); cover and refrigerate.

• Make Sweet Potato Salad; cover and refrigerate.

• Prepare Cabbage-and-Cilantro Slaw through step 1 and refrigerate vegetables and dressing separately.

I N THE SOUTH, BIG ANNUAL FAMILY REUNIONS are serious business (and lots of fun). Pavilions in public parks are booked months in advance, huge smokers are rented, charcoal stockpiled, potluck dishes assigned via circulating Excel spreadsheets.

Here's a hearty, crowd-pleasing meal for a big family get-together. Double or triple the recipes as needed, or add dishes from the other summer menus in this book. If you're the host or organizer, don't be shy about asking aunts and uncles you barely know to bring their favorite picnic sides.

After all this amazing food, you and the family will probably want to either nap or work some of those calories off. Hang up a hammock and have comfy lawn chairs available. Set up horseshoes, cornhole, or a badminton or volleyball net for the more active among you.

- Make Watermelon Limeade and refrigerate.

- Shape burgers, stack between waxed paper to separate them, cover with plastic, and refrigerate.

- Chill beer.

- Rinse lettuce leaves for burgers, pat dry, wrap in paper towels, and put in a plastic bag in the fridge.

UP TO 4 HOURS IN ADVANCE

- Make Blueberry Cobbler; set aside to cool to room temperature.

2 HOURS IN ADVANCE

- Make Baked Macaroni; cover with foil to keep warm.

- Finish slaw.

- Put beer in an ice bucket.

- Slice tomatoes, onions, and cheese for burgers.

1 HOUR IN ADVANCE

- Set out burger fixings.

- Finish chicken thighs and cover with foil to keep warm.

- Finish collards.

- Prepare charcoal fire and grill burgers.

BBQ CHICKEN THIGHS

INGREDIENTS

½ cup granulated sugar

½ cup sea salt

4 tablespoons chili powder

2 tablespoons garlic powder

4 tablespoons ground black pepper

16 skin-on chicken thighs

3 tablespoons butter

1 cup ketchup

½ cup apple cider vinegar

3 tablespoons molasses

3 tablespoons dark brown sugar

2 tablespoons Worcestershire sauce

1 tablespoon mustard

1 tablespoon salt

Tabasco sauce, to taste

THESE CHICKEN THIGHS COMBINE ALL OF THE CLASSIC FLAVORS—SMOKY, SPICY, SWEET, AND TANGY—THAT LOVERS OF GOOD OLD-FASHIONED BARBECUE CRAVE.

1. To make dry rub, combine granulated sugar, sea salt, chili powder, and garlic powder with 2 tablespoons pepper in medium bowl. On large rimmed baking sheet, arrange chicken and rub each piece with dry rub, coating thoroughly. Cover pan tightly with plastic wrap; refrigerate overnight.

2. To make barbecue sauce, melt butter in medium saucepan over medium heat. Add the rest of the ingredients and the remaining 2 tablespoons pepper and stir to combine. Reduce heat to low and simmer, stirring occasionally, 5 to 8 minutes.

3. Preheat oven to 300°F. Meanwhile, remove chicken from refrigerator and let sit at room temperature 10 minutes. Transfer pan to oven and bake 30 minutes.

4. Remove pan and brush chicken liberally with sauce. Increase heat to 400°F and return pan to oven. Continue baking chicken, brushing with sauce once or twice more, until an instant-read thermometer reaches 165°F when inserted into largest piece of chicken and skin is nicely browned and caramelized, 15 to 20 minutes more. Serve remaining barbecue sauce on the side.

EACH SERVING: About 813 calories, 63g protein, 37g carbohydrate, 45g total fat (14g saturated), 376mg cholesterol, 8,509mg sodium

COLLARDS WITH PICKLED RED ONIONS

⤙ SERVES 16

INGREDIENTS

- 2 medium red onions, thinly sliced
- ⅓ cup red wine vinegar
- 2 tablespoons sugar
- ⅛ teaspoon coarsely ground black pepper
- ¾ teaspoon salt
- 2 tablespoons olive oil
- ¼ teaspoon crushed red pepper
- 5 pounds collard greens, stems removed and discarded, leaves coarsely chopped

1. In 3-quart saucepan, heat 2 quarts water to boiling over high heat. Add onion slices and heat to boiling; cook 2 minutes. Drain onions. Rinse onions with cold running water; drain well.

2. Meanwhile, in medium bowl, mix vinegar, sugar, black pepper, and ¼ teaspoon salt until blended. Add onions and toss to mix. Cover and refrigerate at least 4 hours or up to 24 hours.

3. About 20 minutes before serving, in 8-quart pot, heat oil and crushed red pepper over medium-high heat until hot. Gradually add collard greens and cook 10 to 15 minutes or until wilted and tender, stirring frequently. Stir in remaining ½ teaspoon salt.

4. Transfer collard greens to serving bowl. With slotted spoon, remove pickled onions from bowl and arrange over greens.

EACH SERVING: About 50 calories, 2g protein, 7g carbohydrate, 2g total fat (0g saturated), 0mg cholesterol, 105mg sodium

GREEN BEANS WITH TOASTED BENNE SEEDS

⇥| SERVES 10

INGREDIENTS

2 tablespoons olive oil

1½ tablespoons lemon juice

½ tablespoon Dijon mustard

½ teaspoon salt

2 pounds green beans, ends trimmed

1 tablespoon sesame seeds (benne seeds), toasted

THIS IS A PRETTY SALAD THAT CAN BE MADE IN ADVANCE, THEN TOSSED WITH TOASTED BENNE SEEDS (SESAME SEEDS TO NORTHERNERS) JUST BEFORE SERVING.

1. Prepare dressing: In small bowl, with wire whisk or fork, mix oil, lemon juice, mustard, and salt until blended and slightly thickened.

2. In 8-quart Dutch oven over high heat, bring 1 inch water to a boil. Add green beans and return to a boil. Reduce heat to low; cover and simmer 5 to 10 minutes, until beans are tender.

3. Remove beans to colander to drain well.

4. In large bowl, toss warm beans with dressing; cover and refrigerate until ready to serve. Toss beans with sesame seeds just before serving.

EACH SERVING: About 60 calories, 2g protein, 7g carbohydrate, 3g total fat (0g saturated), 0mg cholesterol, 135mg sodium

SWEET POTATO SALAD WITH LEMONY BUTTERMILK DRESSING

SERVES 12

INGREDIENTS

- 3 pounds sweet potatoes (3 large), peeled and cut into 1-inch chunks
- 1 lemon
- ⅔ cup buttermilk
- ¼ cup light mayonnaise
- Salt and coarsely ground black pepper
- 3 stalks celery, thinly sliced
- ¼ cup minced red onion
- ¼ cup loosely packed fresh parsley leaves, chopped

THIS GORGEOUS, TANGY SALAD IS A HEALTHFUL, SOUTHERN-INFLECTED ALTERNATIVE TO THE USUAL POTATO SALAD.

1. In 6-quart saucepan, place potatoes and enough water to cover; heat to boiling over high heat. Reduce heat to medium-low; cover and simmer 8 minutes or until potatoes are just tender.

2. Meanwhile, from lemon, grate 1 teaspoon peel and squeeze 1 tablespoon juice. In large bowl, whisk lemon peel and juice with buttermilk, mayonnaise, ½ teaspoon salt, and ¼ teaspoon pepper. Stir in celery, onion, and parsley.

3. Drain potatoes; cool 10 minutes. Add to dressing in bowl and gently stir until potatoes are well coated. Spoon potato salad into large container with tight-fitting lid. Can be refrigerated up to 1 day.

EACH SERVING: About 130 calories, 2g protein, 26g carbohydrate, 2g total fat (1g saturated), 2mg cholesterol, 170mg sodium

BUTTERMILK

TRUE OLD-TIMEY BUTTERMILK, of course, is the low- or nonfat liquid that's left over after making cultured butter. The buttermilk that you can purchase at any grocery store—and the kind that I assume you'll use here—is milk to which a culture has been added so that it thickens and becomes acidic. I honestly don't know many people under the age of sixty who regularly drink buttermilk straight, but it is an absolutely indispensible ingredient in everything from biscuits and cornbread (it adds a slight tang and reacts with chemical leavening to produce fluffy and light baked goods) to slaws and salad dressings.

CABBAGE-&-CILANTRO SLAW

SERVES 8

INGREDIENTS

- ½ medium head green cabbage
- ¾ cup thinly sliced white onion
- ½ cup fresh cilantro
- ¼ cup vegetable oil
- 3 tablespoons (about 1½ limes) fresh lime juice
- 1 tablespoon apple cider vinegar
- 2 teaspoon freshly ground pepper
- Salt, to taste

THIS SLAW FROM *COUNTRY LIVING* READER ADALE SHOLOCK IS SIMPLE AND DELICIOUS. A GENEROUS AMOUNT OF CILANTRO GIVES IT AN INCREDIBLY FRESH AND VIBRANT CHARACTER.

1. In large bowl, combine cabbage, onion, and cilantro. In medium bowl, whisk oil, lime juice, and vinegar to combine.

2. Sprinkle cabbage mixture with pepper, season with salt, and toss with dressing to combine.

EACH SERVING: About 84 calories, 1g protein, 5g carbohydrate, 7g total fat (1g saturated), 0mg cholesterol, 11mg sodium

BAKED MACARONI

INGREDIENTS

Butter, for greasing baking dish

4 cups (about 1 pound) grated Cheddar cheese

1 can (10¾ ounces) condensed cream of mushroom soup

¾ cup mayonnaise

½ cup chopped onion

1 jar (4 ounces) pimentos, drained and chopped

2 cups elbow macaroni, cooked according to package instructions and drained

2 cups cheese crackers, such as Cheez-It, coarsely crumbled

THE CRUMBLED CHEESE CRACKERS ON TOP OF THIS BAKED PASTA DISH ADD A LITTLE CRUNCH AND EXTRA SAVORY FLAVOR TO MAKE IT IRRESISTIBLE.

1. Preheat oven to 350°F. Meanwhile, butter a 9" by 13" baking dish and set aside.

2. In large bowl, combine the cheese, soup, mayonnaise, onion, and pimentos. Add cooked macaroni; stir to combine.

3. Transfer macaroni mixture to prepared baking dish. Layer crumbled crackers evenly atop casserole. Bake until cheese is bubbly and top of casserole is lightly toasted, about 40 minutes.

EACH SERVING: About 652 calories, 22g protein, 42g carbohydrate, 44g total fat (16g saturated), 72mg cholesterol, 1,008mg sodium

JUMBO PECAN-DATE OATMEAL COOKIES

MAKES 2 DOZEN

INGREDIENTS

- 1 cup (2 sticks) butter or margarine, softened
- ¾ cup granulated sugar
- ¾ cup packed light brown sugar
- 1½ cups all-purpose flour
- 1 teaspoon baking soda
- 1 teaspoon vanilla extract
- ½ teaspoon salt
- ½ teaspoon ground cinnamon
- 2 large eggs
- 3 cups raw quick-cooking oats
- 2 cups (10 ounces) pitted dates, chopped
- 1 cup pecans, chopped

THESE COOKIES TRAVEL WELL—PACK THEM IN AN AIRTIGHT CONTAINER OR IN ZIP-TIGHT PLASTIC BAGS.

1. In large bowl, with mixer on medium speed, beat butter and both sugars until light and fluffy, about 5 minutes. Reduce speed to low; add flour, baking soda, vanilla, salt, cinnamon, and eggs; beat just until blended, occasionally scraping bowl with rubber spatula. With spoon, stir in oats, dates, and pecans.

2. Preheat oven to 350°F. Drop cookie dough by level ¼ cups, 3 inches apart, on two ungreased large cookie sheets.

3. Place cookie sheets on two oven racks. Bake cookies 20 to 25 minutes until golden, rotating cookie sheets between upper and lower racks halfway through baking time. With metal spatula, remove cookies to wire racks to cool.

4. Repeat until all dough is used. Store cookies, tightly covered, up to 1 week.

EACH SERVING: About 400 calories, 4g protein, 35g carbohydrate, 12g total fat (2g saturated), 18mg cholesterol, 205mg sodium

NECTARINE & BLUEBERRY COBBLER

⇥| SERVES 8

INGREDIENTS

FRUIT FILLING

- 8 medium firm but ripe nectarines, pitted and cut into ½-inch wedges
- 1 pint blueberries
- ½ cup sugar
- 1 tablespoon plus 1 teaspoon cornstarch
- 1 tablespoon fresh lemon juice

BISCUIT TOPPING

- 1¾ cups all-purpose flour
- 1 tablespoon baking powder
- ¼ teaspoon salt
- 4 tablespoons sugar
- 1 cup heavy or whipping cream
- Vanilla ice cream (optional)

TART-SWEET, DENSE NECTARINES AND JUICY BLUEBERRIES COMBINE BEAUTIFULLY IN THIS EASY, BISCUIT-TOPPED COBBLER.

1. Prepare fruit filling: In 4-quart saucepan, combine nectarines, blueberries, sugar, cornstarch, lemon juice, and ½ cup water; heat to boiling over medium-high heat, stirring constantly. Reduce heat to low; simmer 2 minutes or until fruit softens. Remove from heat.

2. Prepare biscuit topping: Preheat oven to 450°F. In large bowl, stir together flour, baking powder, salt, and 3 tablespoons sugar. Reserve 1 tablespoon cream for brushing on biscuits later. In medium bowl, with mixer on medium speed, beat remaining cream just until stiff peaks form. With rubber spatula, stir whipped cream into flour mixture just until soft dough forms. With lightly floured hands, knead dough in bowl three or four times, just until it holds together. Do not overmix.

3. Turn dough onto lightly floured surface. With floured rolling pin, roll dough to ¾-inch thickness. With floured 2½-inch round biscuit cutter, cut out as many biscuits as possible. Press trimmings together; reroll and cut to make 8 biscuits in all.

4. Reheat filling to boiling over medium heat. Pour into 11" by 7" ceramic or glass baking dish or shallow 2½-quart casserole.

5. Arrange biscuits on top of fruit mixture; brush with reserved cream and sprinkle with remaining 1 tablespoon sugar.

6. Bake cobbler 15 to 17 minutes, until biscuits are browned and fruit mixture is bubbling. Cool cobbler on wire rack 30 minutes to serve warm, or cool completely to serve later. Serve with ice cream if you like.

EACH SERVING: About 355 calories, 5g protein, 60g carbohydrate, 12g total fat (7g saturated), 41mg cholesterol, 235mg sodium

WATERMELON LIMEADE

⇥ SERVES 8

INGREDIENTS

- 14 cups watermelon cut into 1-inch chunks
- 1 cup fresh lime juice (from 8 to 10 limes)
- ¼ cup sugar, plus more as desired

THIS REFRESHING DRINK USES ONLY THREE INGREDIENTS, MAKING IT EASY TO WHIP UP ON A HOT DAY.

In blender, working in batches, puree watermelon, lime juice, and sugar until smooth. Taste and add more sugar if desired; serve chilled.

EACH SERVING: About 102 calories, 1g protein, 32g carbohydrate, 0g total fat (0g saturated), 0mg cholesterol, 9mg sodium

5

FATHER'S DAY BACKYARD CAMPOUT

Pimento Cheese Dogs

Fried Catfish

Quick Bourbon-Pickled Jalapeños

Buttermilk Cornbread

Corn on the cob

Red Velvet Cupcakes with Creole Cream Cheese Frosting

Bellini Moonshiners

Root beer & lemon water

TIMELINE

3 WEEKS IN ADVANCE

• Make pickled jalapeños; refrigerate.

3 DAYS IN ADVANCE

• Make pimento cheese (step 1 of Pimento Cheese Dogs); cover and refrigerate.

UP TO 1 DAY IN ADVANCE

• Make the Red Velvet Cupcakes; put in a single layer in a container with a lid and refrigerate.

• Find sticks and sharpen for roasting hot dogs.

UP TO 6 HOURS IN ADVANCE

• Ready a charcoal fire (don't light it yet); twist newspaper for kindling.

• Make the Buttermilk Cornbread.

• Chill root beer. Chill sparkling water and Champagne.

2 HOURS IN ADVANCE

• Prepare corn: Pull corn husks down toward the stalk and remove silks, then fold husks back over the cobs. Put in a bucket and cover with cold water to soak.

I HONESTLY DIDN'T KNOW THE FATHER'S DAY CAMPOUT in the yard was a thing until our neighbors told us they'd recently started practicing the tradition. It sure sounds like a good event for early summer whether you're a father, a mother, a kid, or a kid at heart. Father's Day proper is the third Sunday in June, but why not make it a weekend-long celebration and pitch the tent on Saturday? If the weather's going to be especially nice—cooler at night, not too dewy in the morning—try forgoing the tent and sleeping out under the stars.

Of course the best part about a backyard campout is the campfire, so I've built the menu around a few easy things that you can cook over wood: hot dogs (find straight green sticks to sharpen up), corn on the cob (desilked but still in the husks; you can nestle them right in the coals), and catfish fried up in a skillet. Rustle up some bricks or big rocks to arrange around the fire and put the grate from your kettle grill or smoker on them to hold the skillet: instant outdoor stovetop.

• Make Bellini Moonshiners through step 2; refrigerate.

UP TO 1 HOUR IN ADVANCE

• Put root beer on ice, slice a lemon into a drink dispenser and fill with ice water.

• Gather plates, napkins, pot holders, and benches or chairs and a work surface near the fire site. Slice cornbread.

• Prepare catfish fillets through step 1 and refrigerate.

• Set out hot dog buns, pimento cheese, and pickled jalapeños.

DURING THE COOKOUT

• Finish and enjoy Bellini Moonshiners.

• Start fire. When embers are glowing, drain corn and bury in coals until husks darken in spots; turn with tongs so they cook evenly.

• Set a grill grate and skillet over coals and fry catfish.

• Spear hot dogs with sticks so kids can roast them over the fire.

PIMENTO CHEESE DOGS

INGREDIENTS

- 2¼ cups shredded Cheddar cheese
- 6 tablespoons minced jarred pimentos
- 6 tablespoons mayonnaise
- ¾ teaspoon hot sauce
- 6 hot dogs, cooked over a fire or grilled
- 6 hot dog buns

THESE DOGS ARE A WHOLE NEW WAY TO DRESS UP THIS SUMMER STAPLE.

1. Combine cheese, pimentos, mayonnaise, and hot sauce; refrigerate until ready to serve.

2. Divide pimento cheese among hot dogs on buns.

EACH SERVING: About 581 calories, 22g protein, 26g carbohydrate, 43g total fat (18g saturated), 84mg cholesterol, 1,136mg sodium

FRIED CATFISH

SERVES 6

INGREDIENTS

¾ cup cornmeal

2 tablespoons all-purpose flour

½ teaspoon salt

¼ teaspoon ground black pepper

¼ cup milk

6 catfish fillets (6 ounces each)

4 tablespoons vegetable oil

Lemon wedges

BEFORE FRYING, LET THE COATED FISH FILLETS STAND FOR A LITTLE WHILE TO SET THE CRUST; IT WILL ADHERE BETTER AND FRY TO CRISPY PERFECTION.

1. In zip-tight plastic bag, combine cornmeal, flour, salt, and pepper. Pour milk into pie plate. Dip catfish fillets, one at a time, into milk to coat well, then into cornmeal mixture, shaking bag to coat fish. Place coated catfish on wire rack set over waxed paper; set aside to dry 20 minutes.

2. Over a campfire with a grill grate (or on a stovetop over medium-high heat), heat 2 tablespoons oil in a 10-inch skillet until hot. Add 3 catfish fillets to skillet and fry until just opaque throughout and golden, 4 to 5 minutes per side. Transfer to paper towels to drain. Repeat with remaining 2 tablespoons oil and remaining catfish. Serve with lemon wedges.

EACH SERVING: About 377 calories, 28g protein, 16g carbohydrate, 22g total fat (4g saturated), 58mg cholesterol, 235mg sodium

QUICK BOURBON-PICKLED JALAPEÑOS

⫶ MAKES 1 (2-QUART) JAR

INGREDIENTS

- 1 **pound jalapeño peppers, sliced into ½-inch rounds**
- 1¼ **cups distilled white vinegar**
- 1 **cup bourbon**
- ½ **cup honey**
- 2 **teaspoons coriander seeds**
- 1 **teaspoon salt**
- 1 **teaspoon yellow mustard seeds**
- 2 **bay leaves**

SWEET MEETS HEAT IN THESE HONEY-BOURBON-SOAKED PEPPERS. LOUISVILLE, KENTUCKY, CHEF EDWARD LEE KEEPS THESE PICKLES IN THE FRIDGE. "THESE ARE SO GOOD, THEY WON'T LAST LONG ANYWAY."

1. Put jalapeños in clean 2-quart screw-top jar.

2. In small saucepan, combine vinegar, bourbon, honey, coriander seeds, salt, mustard seeds, and bay leaves. Bring to a boil; then simmer 5 minutes.

3. Pour hot liquid over jalapeños and seal jar with tight-fitting lid. Let cool to room temperature. Once cool, refrigerate at least 3 days before serving. (Jalapeño pickles can be stored in refrigerator up to 2 weeks.)

EACH SERVING: About 76 calories, 0g protein, 11g carbohydrate, 0g total fat, 0mg cholesterol, 147mg sodium

BUTTERMILK CORNBREAD

INGREDIENTS

1½ cups coarse cornmeal
(see Note)

1 cup all-purpose flour

1½ teaspoons kosher salt

1 teaspoon baking soda

3 large eggs

1½ cups buttermilk

½ cup (1 stick) unsalted
butter, melted, plus more
for greasing pan

RICH AND SWEET WITH A TENDER CRUMB, THIS BUTTERMILK CORNBREAD FROM STEVEN SATTERFIELD—THE CHEF AT MILLER UNION, IN ATLANTA—IS THE IDEAL ACCOMPANIMENT TO ANY TRADITIONAL SOUTHERN MEAL.

1. Preheat oven to 350°F. In medium bowl, whisk together cornmeal, flour, salt, and baking soda. In a separate bowl, whisk eggs. Add buttermilk. Stir egg mixture into cornmeal mixture, then stir in melted butter. Whisk until ingredients are combined.

2. Butter a 9" by 13" baking pan. Pour cornbread batter into prepared pan and bake until a toothpick inserted in the center tests clean, about 25 minutes. Transfer to a wire rack and let cool before slicing.

EACH SERVING: About 229 calories, 6g protein, 25g carbohydrate, 12g total fat (7g saturated), 89mg cholesterol, 697mg sodium

NOTE: Chef Satterfield says his cornbread has evolved somewhat since this recipe was published; among other changes, now he uses fine cornmeal and no flour. Feel free to make the switch yourself, if you'd like, and use 2½ cups fine cornmeal in place of the coarse cornmeal and flour.

RED VELVET CUPCAKES WITH CREOLE CREAM CHEESE FROSTING

⊰ MAKES 12

INGREDIENTS

- 1⅓ cups all-purpose flour
- 2 tablespoons unsweetened cocoa powder
- ¾ teaspoon baking powder
- ¼ teaspoon baking soda
- ¼ teaspoon salt
- 1 stick (½ cup) unsalted butter, softened
- ¾ cup sugar
- 2 large eggs
- ½ cup buttermilk
- 1 tablespoon liquid red food coloring
- 1 teaspoon vanilla extract
- ½ teaspoon distilled white vinegar
- Red sanding sugar (optional)

FROSTING

- 8 ounces Creole cream cheese (or one 8-ounce package softened cream cheese with 1 teaspoon lemon juice stirred in), softened
- 4 tablespoons (½ stick) unsalted butter, softened
- 1½ cups confectioners' sugar, sifted
- ½ teaspoon vanilla extract

TANGY CREOLE CREAM CHEESE TOPS THESE MOIST RED VELVET CUPCAKES, WHICH ARE EASY TO MAKE FOR PARTIES AND POTLUCKS TOO.

1. Prepare cupcakes: Preheat oven to 350°F. Line 12-cup muffin pan with paper liners. In small bowl, whisk flour, cocoa, baking powder, baking soda, and salt. In large bowl, with electric mixer on medium speed, beat butter and sugar until light and creamy. Beat in eggs, one at a time. In glass measure, combine buttermilk, food coloring, vanilla, and vinegar. With mixer on low, beat in flour mixture in thirds, alternating with buttermilk mixture, until blended. Beat 2 minutes, scraping bowl occasionally, until batter is smooth. Divide batter evenly among muffin cups.

2. Bake 18 to 22 minutes, until a toothpick inserted into cupcakes comes out clean. Let cool in pan 5 minutes before removing to a wire rack to cool completely.

3. Prepare frosting: In large bowl, with electric mixer on medium speed, beat cream cheese and butter until well blended. Add confectioners' sugar and vanilla and beat until smooth and fluffy. Frost cupcakes and refrigerate to firm up frosting. Sprinkle with red sanding sugar, if desired. Bring to room temperature before serving.

EACH SERVING: About 343 calories, 5g protein, 40g carbohydrate, 19g total fat (11g saturated), 83mg cholesterol, 203mg sodium

RED VELVET

Red velvet cake may not have originated in the South (its history is murky and involves the Waldorf-Astoria in New York, of all places), but it fits so snugly into the southern cake tradition that you'd be hard-pressed these days to find a southern bakery that didn't offer some version of it or a southern home baker who didn't have a favored recipe. True red velvet cake should have a very fine, tender crumb (this is where "velvet" comes in) and should be a deep, rich, dark burgundy, not bright red. Cream cheese frosting is not historically accurate—apparently early red velvet cakes were iced with a frosting made from a boiled milk-and-flour slurry that was beaten into butter and sugar—but in my opinion the tangier the frosting the better, so cream cheese it is.

BELLINI MOONSHINERS

INGREDIENTS

2 ripe peaches, peeled, pitted, and quartered

32 fresh basil leaves, plus 8 more for garnish

½ cup confectioners' sugar

Juice of 2 limes (about ¼ cup)

1½ cups moonshine, such as Prichard's Lincoln County Lightning

4 cups ice

1 liter sparkling water

1 bottle (750 ml) champagne

ALABAMA CHEF DAVID BANCROFT DEVISED BELLINI MOONSHINERS, A HIGH-LOW MIX OF FANCY CHAMPAGNE AND LINCOLN COUNTY LIGHTNING WHISKEY. FRESH PEACHES AND BASIL ADD A TASTE OF SUMMER.

1. In large jug, muddle peaches, basil, and sugar using a muddler or the back of a wooden spoon.

2. Add lime juice and moonshine and stir well.

3. Add 4 cups ice. To serve, divide mixture evenly among eight high-ball glasses and top off with sparkling water and champagne. Garnish each glass with a basil leaf and serve immediately.

EACH SERVING: About 211 calories, 0g protein, 14g carbohydrate, 0g total fat, 0mg cholesterol, 1mg sodium

SPRINKLER PARTY

Crispy Fried Chicken

Down-home Peach Ice Cream

Magnolia's Lemonade

Watermelon

Fresh figs & scuppernong grapes

TIMELINE

UP TO 1 DAY IN ADVANCE

• Make Magnolia's Lemonade, adding just 6 cups cold water; refrigerate.

• Prepare the ice cream through step 3.

• Set up sprinklers and hose, gather water guns, water balloons, and so on.

THE NIGHT BEFORE

• Make sure you have plenty of ice and ice cream salt if using an old-fashioned churn. If churning in advance, do that now and put the ice cream in an airtight container in the freezer.

CASUAL ENTERTAINING AT ITS BEST, this one's mostly for the kiddos (although I'd be surprised if at least a few adults didn't end up running through the spray of cold water, too). While a simple lawn sprinkler or two will entertain your average child for hours, consider more elaborate variations of outdoor water fun. Friends of ours who lived on some acreage outside Athens, Georgia, made a homemade slide that ran down a steep hill and into a pit they'd dug out, lined with a tarp, and filled with water; they'd rub the sheet-metal slide with waxed paper to make it super-slippery, then turn on a hose at the top. Similar results can be had with a roll of heavy-duty plastic, a water source, and a sloping yard.

Good fried chicken is good at any temperature, so make it in advance and set it out in a big bucket or on a platter for stand-up eating. If your kids are up to the task, you can have them take turns turning the crank on the ice cream churn. Cut up a couple of watermelons, have the kids raid the fig trees and scuppernong vines, and provide plenty of cold lemonade. No plates or napkins necessary, but you'll want to serve the soft ice cream in bowls.

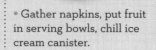

• Prepare Crispy Fried Chicken through step 1; refrigerate overnight.

2 HOURS IN ADVANCE

• Cut up watermelon.

• Rinse figs and scuppernongs.

• Gather napkins, put fruit in serving bowls, chill ice cream canister.

• Dredge and fry the chicken. Serve hot or at room temperature within 2 hours.

LAST 30 MINUTES

• Churn the ice cream out in the yard with the kids' help. Serve in bowls with spoons (it'll be soft).

• Add 6 cups ice to lemonade and serve.

CRISPY FRIED CHICKEN

INGREDIENTS

- 1 (4-pound) chicken, cut into 8 pieces
- 3 cups buttermilk
- 1 tablespoon kosher salt
- 1 tablespoon hot red pepper sauce
- 2 cups all-purpose flour
- 1 tablespoon garlic powder
- 1 tablespoon onion powder
- 2 teaspoons ground black pepper
- 6 cups canola oil

ENJOY THE ULTIMATE COMFORT FOOD: CLASSIC CRISPY FRIED CHICKEN.

1. Place chicken in large food storage bag. Add buttermilk, salt, and hot sauce. Seal bag; turn bag to coat chicken. Refrigerate overnight.

2. In large plastic bag, combine flour, garlic powder, onion powder, and pepper; close bag and shake to mix. Drain chicken; add a few pieces of chicken at a time to bag and shake to coat. Place chicken on waxed paper.

3. In a 12-inch cast-iron skillet or a heavy pot with a deep-fat thermometer attached, heat oil (to about a 1-inch depth) to 350°F. Preheat oven to 200°F.

4. In batches, to avoid overcrowding, fry chicken 12 to 14 minutes or until internal temperature registers 175°F on an instant-read thermometer. Drain chicken on paper towels, then transfer to a wire rack set over a baking sheet and keep warm in oven while frying remaining batches.

EACH SERVING: About 907 calories, 65g protein, 28g carbohydrate, 58g total fat (9g saturated), 173mg cholesterol, 455mg sodium

DOWN-HOME PEACH ICE CREAM

SERVES 10

INGREDIENTS

- 1 medium lemon
- 6 medium ripe peaches (about 2 pounds)
- ¾ cup sugar
- 1 cup heavy cream
- 1 cup milk
- 1 piece vanilla bean (about 2 inches long), split in half
- ⅛ teaspoon salt

AN OLD-FASHIONED TREAT FOR THE WHOLE FAMILY—SWEET HOMEMADE ICE CREAM WITH SWIRLS OF CRUSHED PEACHES. GET YOUR SPOONS READY!

1. From lemon, finely grate ¼ teaspoon peel and squeeze 1 tablespoon juice. Peel and remove pits from peaches; reserve pits. Cut peaches into chunks

2. In food processor with knife blade attached, combine peaches, sugar, and lemon juice; pulse just to a chunky consistency. Pour peach mixture into bowl; cover and refrigerate until well chilled.

3. Meanwhile, in 2-quart saucepan, combine cream, milk, vanilla bean, salt, lemon peel, and reserved peach pits; heat over medium-high heat just until bubbles form around edge of pan. Pour cream mixture into bowl; cover and refrigerate until well chilled, at least 2 hours.

4. Strain cream mixture through sieve into peach mixture; stir until blended. Pour mixture into ice-cream maker and freeze as manufacturer directs. Serve immediately or place in freezer to harden. Use within 2 weeks.

EACH SERVING: About 185 calories, 2g protein, 25g carbohydrate, 10g total fat (6g saturated), 36mg cholesterol, 35mg sodium

MAGNOLIA'S LEMONADE

SERVES 12

INGREDIENTS

3 cups fresh lemon juice
2 cups sugar
12 cups ice water

THE SIMPLICITY OF A PERFECT GLASS OF LEMONADE—MADE WITH JUST FRESH LEMON JUICE, SUGAR, AND WATER—IS ONE OF SUMMER'S UNRIVALED PLEASURES.

Combine lemon juice, sugar, and 12 cups ice water in a pitcher and stir.

EACH SERVING: About 143 calories, 0g protein, 38g carbohydrate, 0g total fat (0g saturated), 0mg cholesterol, 1mg sodium

COASTAL DINNER PARTY

Zucchini, Leek & Mint Soup

Savannah Red Rice with
Shrimp & Smoked Sausage

Sea Island Red Peas

Double Cornbread

Island Ambrosia

Shredded kale salad with
lemon juice & olive oil

White or rosé wine

TIMELINE

1 WEEK IN ADVANCE
• Make Hot Pepper Vinegar.

UP TO 2 DAYS IN ADVANCE
• Prepare coconut for Island Ambrosia (step 1); cover and refrigerate.

UP TO 1 DAY IN ADVANCE
• Grate zucchini and chop leek for Zucchini, Leek, and Mint Soup; cover and refrigerate.

• Shred or thinly slice kale for salad; cover and refrigerate.

• Chop onion, celery, and garlic for the red rice and refrigerate together.

• Source and prepare fresh shrimp for Savannah Red Rice with Shrimp and Smoked Sausage.

• Peel and devein sausage, cover, and refrigerate.

THE NIGHT BEFORE
• Soak red peas for Sea Island Red Peas.

• Chill wine.

• Prepare pineapple and oranges for ambrosia (steps 2 and 3); cover and refrigerate together.

THIS MENU, WHICH HAPPENS TO BE ORGANIZED around a couple of dishes from one of my favorite southern chefs, Steven Satterfield, is on the fancier end of the dinner-party spectrum (there's a separate soup course!), but that doesn't mean it has to be stiff or formal, and it shouldn't be difficult to pull off. You could even just skip the soup and set out some easy finger foods, like the spiced pecans on page 40 or the cheese straws on page 39. That said, it's a fine excuse to pull out the good china and open a few bottles of special wine.

A coastal party is about enjoying the view and keeping things simple and delicious. It's important to use the best ingredients possible: buy the best Gulf or Georgia shrimp at the last minute, and seek out good-quality heirloom dried beans and rice. Keep the side salad simple, and dress it with plenty of bright lemon juice and maybe a shower of grated Parmesan. The dessert of fresh coconut and tropical fruit is likewise light and refreshing, not too overwhelming for a summer meal.

UP TO 3 HOURS IN ADVANCE

- Set table with soup bowls and plates; set out pepper vinegar.
- Make Double Cornbread.
- Make red peas; reheat just before serving if needed.
- Grill sausage; let cool, slice, then cover and refrigerate.

1 HOUR IN ADVANCE

- Slice the cornbread.
- Finish kale salad: Put kale in salad bowl, season with salt, and massage until wilted. Squeeze fresh lemon juice over kale and drizzle with olive oil. Set on the table.
- Start red rice.

LAST 30 MINUTES

- Finish soup.
- Finish red rice.
- Add coconut to pineapple and oranges and toss to finish ambrosia. Chill until ready to serve.

ZUCCHINI, LEEK & MINT SOUP

······················ SERVES 8

INGREDIENTS

QUICK AND EASY, THIS SOUP IS LIGHT AND FLAVORFUL, AND IDEAL AS A STARTER FOR AN END-OF-SUMMER MEAL.

2 zucchini, grated

2 leeks (white parts only), finely chopped

2 tablespoons finely chopped fresh mint, plus additional sprigs for garnish

5 cups chicken stock

Salt and ground black pepper, to taste

Place the zucchini, leeks, mint, and stock in large saucepan. Bring to a boil, reduce heat, and simmer 20 minutes or until leeks are tender. Puree in a blender (with center part removed to let steam escape) or use an immersion blender. Season with salt and pepper to taste, and garnish with mint sprigs.

EACH SERVING: About 32 calories, 2g protein, 5g carbohydrate, 1g total fat (1g saturated), 3mg cholesterol, 609mg sodium

SAVANNAH RED RICE WITH SHRIMP & SMOKED SAUSAGE

INGREDIENTS

- 4 tablespoons (½ stick) unsalted butter
- ¼ cup bacon fat
- 1 small yellow onion, diced
- 2½ stalks celery, diced (with inner leaves included)
- 2 cloves garlic, minced
- 2 cans (14.5 ounces each) organic plum tomatoes, drained and chopped
- 2 cups chicken stock
- 2 tablespoons homemade Hot Pepper Vinegar (page 78)
- 2 bay leaves
- 2 dried red chiles (such as chiles de arbol), chopped
- ¾ teaspoon dried thyme
- 1 teaspoon ground black pepper
  Kosher salt, to taste
- 2 cups Carolina Gold or basmati rice
- 1 pound shrimp, peeled and deveined
- 1 pound smoked sausage (such as andouille), grilled and sliced into ½-inch-thick pieces

A TRADITIONAL SOUTHERN DISH, RED RICE GETS ITS COLOR FROM LOTS AND LOTS OF TOMATOES—NEARLY TWO POUNDS OF CANNED TOMATOES—IN THIS RECIPE FROM STEVEN SATTERFIELD.

1. In large skillet, melt half the butter and half the bacon fat over medium-high heat. Add onion, celery, and garlic and sauté until tender, about 5 minutes. Add tomatoes, stock, vinegar, bay leaves, chiles, thyme, and pepper and reduce heat to medium-low; simmer about 15 minutes. Season with salt.

2. In large cast-iron skillet, melt remaining butter and bacon fat over medium heat and sauté rice until opaque, 5 to 6 minutes. Add 4 cups tomato mixture and cook, covered, over very low heat, about 30 minutes. Turn off heat and allow rice to rest, covered, for 5 minutes more.

3. In separate pan, sauté shrimp in remaining tomato mixture until tender, about 5 minutes, then add grilled sausage. Fluff rice with a fork and combine with shrimp-and-sausage mixture.

EACH SERVING: About 450 calories, 19g protein, 38g carbohydrate, 24g total fat (8g saturated), 114mg cholesterol, 686mg sodium

HOT PEPPER VINEGAR

INGREDIENTS

- 1 pound assorted small hot peppers (such as jalapeños, serranos, and habaneros)
- 4 cups apple cider vinegar
- 2 tablespoons kosher salt

CHEF STEVEN SATTERFIELD DIVULGES HIS GRANDMOTHER'S RECIPE FOR A FAMILY SPECIALTY, HOT PEPPER VINEGAR. WHEN PICKLING YOUR OWN PRODUCE, BEGIN BY STERILIZING A CLEAN 1-QUART GLASS CANNING JAR AND LID IN A POT OF BOILING WATER FOR 15 MINUTES. USE TONGS TO REMOVE THE LID AND THE JAR, WHICH SHOULD STILL BE HOT WHEN FILLED WITH THE PEPPERS.

1. Fill sterilized jar with hot peppers.

2. In large pot over high heat, bring vinegar and salt to a boil.

3. Remove pot from heat and ladle piping-hot vinegar-salt mixture over peppers; seal jar.

4. Allow jar to sit at least 1 week to marry the flavors before using. Refrigerate after opening.

EACH SERVING: About 3 calories, 0g protein, 0g carbohydrate, 0g total fat (0g saturated), 0mg cholesterol, 181mg sodium

TIP Serve Hot Pepper Vinegar as a condiment to drizzle over greens, fried meats, and rice dishes.

SEA ISLAND RED PEAS

INGREDIENTS

- 1 tablespoon extra-virgin olive oil
- 1 tablespoon unsalted butter
- 2 stalks celery, diced
- 1 small onion, diced
  Kosher salt and ground black pepper, to taste
- 2 cups dried Sea Island red peas or black-eyed peas, soaked overnight, drained, and rinsed
- 2 quarts chicken or vegetable stock

SEA ISLAND RED PEAS ARE A PARTICULAR BRAND OF HEIRLOOM LEGUMES, BUT IF YOU CANNOT GET THEM, YOU CAN EASILY USE BLACK-EYED PEAS INSTEAD.

1. In large heavy-bottomed pot, heat oil and butter over medium-high heat. Add celery and onion and sauté. Season lightly with salt and pepper and cook until vegetables are tender, about 5 minutes.

2. Add peas and stock. Cover and simmer over medium heat until peas are tender, about 1 hour 15 minutes. Season broth with salt and pepper and simmer until peas absorb salt, about 15 minutes more.

EACH SERVING: About 154 calories, 8g protein, 21g carbohydrate, 4g total fat (1g saturated), 3mg cholesterol, 467mg sodium

HEIRLOOM BEANS & GRAINS

SOUTHERN CHEFS, FOLLOWING THE EXAMPLE OF SEAN BROCK, of McCrady's in Charleston and Husk in Nashville, are actively seeking out heirloom ingredients—and not just local tomato and okra varieties. They're using heritage dry goods: rice, corn, and dried bean varieties that just a few years ago were on the verge of extinction due to decades of neglect in favor of modern varieties that could produce more reliably in nutrient-depleted, monocropped southern soils. Thanks to tireless efforts by these chefs and local growers, seed savers, and scientists, the old varieties—in all their flavorful, individual glory, are now much more readily available to home cooks. Check out the selection from Anson Mills, which has been working closely with Brock to reintroduce heirloom strains.

DOUBLE CORNBREAD

INGREDIENTS

1½ cups all-purpose flour

1½ cups yellow cornmeal

¼ cup sugar

4 teaspoons baking powder

½ teaspoon baking soda

1 teaspoon salt

2½ cups buttermilk

3 large eggs

1 package (10 ounces) frozen corn, thawed

6 tablespoons butter or margarine, melted

2 jalapeño chiles, seeds and membranes discarded, finely chopped

FROZEN CORN ENHANCES THE TEXTURE AND FLAVOR OF HEARTY CORNBREAD WITHOUT A LOT OF EXTRA EXPENSE. BAKE AND FREEZE THE CORNBREAD, TIGHTLY WRAPPED, UP TO 1 MONTH AHEAD. THAW; THEN, WHEN READY TO SERVE, REHEAT, COVERED WITH FOIL, AT 450°F FOR 15 MINUTES. CUT INTO SERVING PIECES.

1. Preheat oven to 450°F. Grease 13" by 9" baking pan.

2. In large bowl, combine flour, cornmeal, sugar, baking powder, baking soda, and salt. In medium bowl, with wire whisk or fork, beat buttermilk and eggs until blended.

3. To buttermilk mixture, add corn, melted butter, and jalapeños, then add to flour mixture. Stir until ingredients are just mixed.

4. Pour batter into prepared pan. Bake 22 to 25 minutes or until golden at edges and toothpick inserted in center comes out clean. Cut lengthwise into 4 strips, then cut each strip crosswise into 6 pieces.

EACH SERVING: About 138 calories, 4g protein, 20g carbohydrate, 5g total fat (3g saturated), 34mg cholesterol, 274mg sodium

ISLAND AMBROSIA

INGREDIENTS

1 fresh coconut
1 ripe pineapple
6 large navel oranges

A LIGHT, REFRESHING FRUIT DESSERT. USE A VEGETABLE PEELER TO SHAVE OFF GRACEFUL, THIN STRIPS OF COCONUT.

1. Prepare coconut: Preheat oven to 350°F. With hammer and screwdriver or large nail, puncture two of the three eyes (indentations at one end) of the coconut. Drain liquid. Bake coconut 15 minutes. Remove coconut from oven and wrap in kitchen towel. With hammer, hit coconut to break it into large pieces. With knife, pry coconut meat from shell. With vegetable peeler or sharp paring knife, peel brown outer skin from coconut meat. With vegetable peeler or large holes of grater, peel or grate 1 cup coconut. (Wrap and refrigerate remaining coconut up to 2 days for another use.)

2. Prepare pineapple: Cut off crown and stem end from pineapple. Stand pineapple upright on cutting board and, with large chef's knife, slice off rind and remove eyes. Cut pineapple lengthwise into quarters. Cut out core. Cut quarters lengthwise in half; slice into chunks. Place in large bowl.

3. Prepare oranges: Cut off ends from oranges; place on a cut end on cutting board and slice off rind. Holding oranges over bowl, with paring knife, cut out sections. Squeeze juice from membranes into bowl.

4. Add shredded coconut to bowl and toss gently to combine.

EACH SERVING: About 120 calories, 2g protein, 24g carbohydrate, 3g total fat (2g saturated), 0mg cholesterol, 3mg sodium

FALL

GATHERING FAMILY

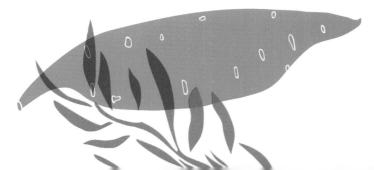

FALL MAY BE more conventionally gorgeous in the North, where colorful foliage is pretty much guaranteed, but after the dog days of a southern August (which often extend into September) even the slightest hint of a cool breeze is reason to celebrate. Of course, when the local football team is playing at home, or anywhere within a three-state radius, it doesn't matter what the weather's like: big cuts of pork will meet smoke, pimentos will meld with cheese and mayo, beer will be nestled into ice at a classic **Tailgate**.

Early fall is also the time to rush the last of the garden and farmers' market produce into storage for the winter and use for **A Traditional Thanksgiving**. In Georgia, we'd take day trips up to the mountains for the best apples to make into applesauce, and scour the roadsides for muscadines to can or freeze. Not-yet-ripe tomatoes would be plucked just before the frost and pickled for the pantry. And I still miss the sound of pecans falling onto the old tin roof of our house in the country. Any of these would be a fine excuse to have friends over for an informal meal: Do some canning or pecan-shelling together, then gather at the kitchen table and celebrate a productive afternoon with an easy supper pulled from the oven or ladled from a slow cooker, and follow up with some **Fireside Drinks**.

WHAT'S IN SEASON

Apples

Broccoli

Collard greens

Kale

Muscadines & scuppernongs

Pecans

Sweet potatoes

Tomatillos & green tomatoes

8

TAILGATE

**Easy Carolina
Pork-Shoulder Sandwiches**

Memphis Ribs

Honey-Baked Beans

**Chopped Collard & Kale Salad
with Lemon-Garlic Dressing**

Fresh Apple Cake

Apple Cider Punch

TIMELINE

2 DAYS IN ADVANCE

• Prepare the Memphis Ribs through step 1.

1 DAY IN ADVANCE

• Continue ribs through step 2; let cool, cover, and refrigerate.

• Make the rub and sauce for the pork shoulder (steps 1 and 2); refrigerate sauce.

• Chop cabbage for pork sandwiches and refrigerate.

• Make Honey-Baked Beans; refrigerate in flame-proof cooking pot.

• Make Fresh Apple Cake; let cool, then wrap in plastic. Pack a container of confectioners' sugar for dusting after you unwrap.

• Prepare ingredients for collard and kale salad: Chop collards and kale, cut corn, hard-cook eggs, and cook bacon; refrigerate.

• Make sure you have plenty of ice for coolers and punch.

• Chill rum.

YOU DON'T HAVE TO BE OBSESSED WITH FOOTBALL to throw a kicking tailgate party (in a parking lot near the stadium or at home in your driveway), but if you aren't a fan don't say so too emphatically on Game Day unless you want to be drawn into an hours-long discussion ranging from the physical beauty of the game itself, to the history of the local team, to detailed prognostications regarding the current contest. In towns with SEC teams especially, it's just assumed that you're a booster unless you (foolishly) state otherwise.

What follows is a fairly typical food lineup for a fall Saturday afternoon. If you'd like, bake up a batch of cornbread (page 63 or 82) to soak up the tangy baked beans and barbecue sauce. The timeline below presents a strategy for an authentic tailgate—where you'd set up a grill in a spot close to the stadium—which complicates food preparation because much of it needs to be transported. It'd be much simpler, of course, to just turn on the game and "tailgate" at home.

• Gather lump charcoal, tongs, pot holders, cutting board, knife. Gather serving gear: platters, salad bowl, serving utensils, plates and forks, punch cups. Put wood chips in sealable container and cover with water to soak.

MORNING OF THE TAILGATE

• Pack dampened towels in plastic bags for cleanup.

• Butter cut sides of buns and pack for transport.

• Make Apple Cider Punch through step 1 and put on ice. Pack sparkling cider and sliced apple for garnish.

• Add BBQ sauce to cabbage (step 3 of sandwich recipe).

• Make dressing for salad and put it in cooler with ice for transport, along with the rest of the prepared salad ingredients.

• Put ribs and extra sauce for pork on ice.

DURING THE TAILGATE

• Smoke and chop pork shoulder. Toast buns.

• Reheat ribs and baked beans on the grill.

• Finish salad.

• Unwrap cake, dust with confectioners' sugar.

EASY CAROLINA PORK-SHOULDER SANDWICHES

INGREDIENTS

- 2 tablespoons kosher salt, plus more to taste
- 2 tablespoons black pepper, plus more to taste
- 2 tablespoons sweet paprika
- 2 tablespoons dry mustard
- 2 tablespoons plus 1 cup dark brown sugar
- 1 cup prepared mustard
- 1 cup vinegar
- 1 small head cabbage, cored and chopped
- 12 sesame buns
  Melted butter, for brushing
- 1 (7- to 8-pound) pork shoulder (aka Boston butt)
  Wood chips soaked in water or beer

IMPRESS YOUR TAILGATE-MATES WITH THIS DECEPTIVELY SIMPLE SOUTHERN-STYLE SANDWICH RECIPE FROM *BARBECUE BIBLE* AUTHOR STEVEN RAICHLEN. IF YOU'RE SMOKING THE SHOULDER AT HOME, START IT EARLY AND MAKE THE SAUCE AND SLAW WHILE IT COOKS. TRY TO USE LUMP CHARCOAL, WHICH BURNS CLEANER THAN BRIQUETTES.

1. Prepare rub: In small bowl, combine salt, pepper, paprika, dry mustard, and the 2 tablespoons brown sugar. Season pork shoulder with the rub, massaging it into the meat with your fingers.

2. Prepare sauce: Combine prepared mustard, remaining 1 cup brown sugar, and vinegar in saucepan and boil until thick, whisking often, 3 to 5 minutes. Add salt and pepper to taste and let cool to room temperature.

3. Prepare slaw: Stir 1 cup sauce into cabbage in large mixing bowl.

4. Brush insides of buns with melted butter; set aside.

5. Light lump charcoal in a chimney starter. Set up a charcoal grill for indirect grilling and heat it to 350°F. Place the spice-rubbed pork shoulder fat side up in the center of the grate over a foil drip pan, so the dripping fat bastes the meat as it cooks.

6. Toss a handful of soaked wood chips on each mound of coals. Cover grill and indirect-grill pork until it's the color of mahogany and as tender as a broken heart. The internal temperature should register 195°F on an instant-read meat thermometer; it will take 4 to 5 hours. Add fresh charcoal every hour. (Leave the grill lid off for 5 minutes when you do, so the new coals have plenty of air to ignite.) You should also add a handful of soaked wood chips to each mound of coals every hour for the first 3 hours.

EACH SERVING: About 729 calories, 49g protein, 49g carbohydrate, 38g total fat (14g saturated), 172mg cholesterol, 1,552mg sodium

MEMPHIS RIBS

✂ SERVES 8

INGREDIENTS

- 6 tablespoons paprika
- 1 teaspoon cayenne (ground red pepper)
- 1 teaspoon celery salt
- 1 teaspoon dry mustard
- 1 teaspoon ground cumin
- 4 teaspoons packed brown sugar
- 3 teaspoons kosher salt
- 4 teaspoons ground black pepper
- 2 racks (2 to 2½ pounds each) St. Louis–style pork ribs
- 1 cup boiling water

A CLASSIC COUNTRY-STYLE FAVORITE, MEMPHIS RIBS SKIP THE SAUCE IN FAVOR OF A SPICY DRY RUB.

1. Prepare dry rub: In bowl, combine paprika, cayenne, celery salt, dry mustard, cumin, brown sugar, salt, and black pepper. In large roasting pan, place ribs side by side; rub with half the dry rub. (Set the remaining rub aside.) Cover and refrigerate at least 1 hour or up to 1 day.

2. Preheat oven to 350°F. Uncover ribs and add boiling water to pan. Cover pan tightly with foil. Bake 1 hour 30 minutes or until tender. Uncover ribs.

3. Prepare outdoor grill for direct grilling over medium-low heat.

4. Grill ribs, bone side down, 5 minutes, sprinkling with remaining dry rub. Turn ribs over; grill 5 minutes, sprinkling with dry rub. Repeat.

EACH SERVING: About 555 calories, 39g protein, 6g carbohydrate, 41g total fat (15g saturated), 160mg cholesterol, 615mg sodium

HONEY-BAKED BEANS

⟩ SERVES 16

INGREDIENTS

- 6 slices thickly cut bacon, chopped
- 1 large onion, chopped
- 2 large cloves garlic, chopped
- ¼ cup tomato paste
- 2 cups chicken broth
- ⅔ cup brown sugar
- ⅓ cup honey
- ¼ cup sherry vinegar
- 3 tablespoons Dijon mustard
- 1 teaspoon paprika
- 1 teaspoon salt
- ½ teaspoon freshly ground pepper
- 4 cans (15 ounces each) pinto beans, drained and rinsed

OVERNIGHT SOAKING? HOURS OF SIMMERING? FORGET IT. LET THESE READY-TO-EAT WONDERS TRIM TIME OFF YOUR MEAL PREP.

1. Preheat oven to 350°F. Heat large Dutch oven over medium heat. Add bacon and cook until crisp, about 5 minutes.

2. Add onion and garlic and cook until soft, about 6 minutes. Add tomato paste, broth, brown sugar, honey, vinegar, mustard, paprika, salt, and pepper and stir to mix.

3. Stir in beans, increase heat to high, and bring to a boil. Transfer to oven and bake, uncovered, until beans are tender and mixture is thickened, 40 to 45 minutes.

EACH SERVING: About 232 calories, 8g protein, 35g carbohydrate, 8g total fat (0g saturated), 10mg cholesterol, 577mg sodium

CHOPPED COLLARD & KALE SALAD WITH LEMON-GARLIC DRESSING

⇥ SERVES 8

INGREDIENTS

- ½ cup olive oil
- Juice of 2 lemons (about ¼ cup)
- 2 cloves garlic, minced
- 2 teaspoons Dijon mustard
- 1 teaspoon kosher salt
- 1 bunch collard greens, chopped into bite-size pieces
- 1 bunch kale, chopped into bite-size pieces
- 2 avocados, cut into ½-inch cubes
- 4 carrots, peeled and grated
- 4 large hard-boiled eggs, diced
- 2 ears (about 2 cups) corn, kernels removed
- 1 pint cherry tomatoes, halved
- ½ cup pecans, toasted
- 6 strips cooked bacon, crumbled

TOMATOES, PECANS, BACON, AND MORE TOP A HEARTY SALAD OF KALE AND COLLARDS.

1. In medium bowl, whisk together oil, lemon juice, garlic, mustard, and salt. Refrigerate dressing 1 hour.

2. In large bowl, combine remaining ingredients. Toss gently with dressing to coat.

EACH SERVING: About 374 calories, 10g protein, 18g carbohydrate, 31g total fat (5g saturated), 100mg cholesterol, 344mg sodium

FRESH APPLE CAKE

⊰| SERVES 12

INGREDIENTS

- 1 cup chopped walnuts
- 3 cups all-purpose flour
- 1 teaspoon baking soda
- 1 teaspoon salt
- 2 teaspoons vanilla extract
- 1 teaspoon ground cinnamon
- 3½ cups chopped peeled Granny Smith apples (3 medium)
- 2 cups granulated sugar
- 1 cup vegetable oil
- 3 large eggs
- Confectioners' sugar, for dusting

PAULA DEEN COMBINES WALNUTS AND GRANNY SMITH APPLES IN THIS COMFORTING CINNAMON-SPICED CAKE.

1. Preheat oven to 325°F. Coat 10-inch tube pan with removable bottom with nonstick cooking spray with flour.

2. Place walnuts in 15½" by 10½" jelly-roll pan; toast in oven 7 minutes or until golden and fragrant. Cool completely in pan on wire rack. Meanwhile, in large bowl, whisk flour, baking soda, and salt. In another large bowl, combine walnuts, vanilla, cinnamon, and 3 cups apples. Reserve remaining ½ cup apple.

3. In large bowl, with mixer on medium-high speed, beat granulated sugar, oil, and eggs until well blended. With mixer on low speed, gradually add flour mixture, scraping bowl occasionally with rubber spatula. Beat 1 minute longer or until well combined. With spatula, fold in apple mixture (batter will be thick). Spoon batter into prepared pan. Scatter remaining apple over top of batter; with fingers, press into top of batter.

4. Bake 1½ hours or until toothpick inserted in center comes out clean. Cool in pan on wire rack until completely cooled. Unmold cake and transfer to cake plate. Dust cake lightly with confectioners' sugar.

EACH SERVING: About 510 calories, 7g protein, 65g carbohydrate, 26g total fat (3g saturated), 53mg cholesterol, 315mg sodium

APPLE CIDER PUNCH

INGREDIENTS

- ½ gallon apple cider, chilled
- 1 quart white grape juice, chilled
- 8 ounces orange juice
- 8 teaspoons star anise pieces
- 3 large Golden Delicious apples, sliced crosswise
- 1 bottle (750-ml) sparkling apple cider, chilled
- Ice
- 16 ounces dark rum (optional)

1. In a punch bowl or large pitcher, combine apple cider, grape juice, and orange juice. Add star anise and slices from 2 apples.

2. Add sparkling cider.

3. To serve, fill tumblers with ice. Add 1 ounce rum to each glass, if desired, and top with punch. Garnish each with 1 apple slice.

EACH SERVING: About 148 calories, 1g protein, 37g carbohydrate, 0g total fat (0g saturated), 0mg cholesterol, 14mg sodium

A TRADITIONAL THANKSGIVING

No-Baste, No-Bother
Roasted Turkey

Herbed Oyster Stuffing

Sourdough Stuffing with
Sweet Potatoes & Cranberries

Southern-Style Green Beans

Alabama Spoon Bread
with Pumpkin & Chives

Praline Candied Garnet Yams

Cracked-Pepper
Dinner Rolls

Dilly Snap Beans

Sweet Potato Pie with
Buttermilk Ice Cream

Old-Fashioned Pecan Pie

Hummingbird Cake

Mashed potatoes

Cranberry sauce

Red & white wine, cold apple
cider, coffee with dessert

TIMELINE

2 WEEKS TO 2 DAYS IN ADVANCE

• Make the Dilly Snap Beans.

• Make the Buttermilk Ice Cream.

• Make the pie shell dough (double the recipe), wrap in plastic, and refrigerate. (Or freeze up to 2 weeks in advance and thaw in the fridge.)

3 DAYS IN ADVANCE

• Start thawing the turkey if frozen.

2 DAYS IN ADVANCE

• Prebake pie shells; let cool and set aside at room temperature.

• Bake yams for Praline Candied Garnet Yams.

1 DAY IN ADVANCE

• Make cake; cover with cake dome and keep at cool room temperature.

• Make Southern-Style Green Beans; refrigerate.

• Make Cracked-Pepper Dinner Rolls; keep in an airtight container.

• Prepare ingredients for stuffing: dice bread, chop and refrigerate vegetables.

THE NIGHT BEFORE

• Make the pies. Keep at cool room temperature.

• Assemble yams in baking dish, cover, and refrigerate.

Of COURSE, FOODWISE THE BIG EVENT OF THE FALL SEASON is Thanksgiving, and southerners don't hold back. The menu here is a fairly basic one, very close to the Thanksgiving dinners my aunt and uncle in Virginia would host—right down to the famous Dilly Snap Beans. Be sure to flip through the rest of the fall and winter recipes for more seasonal vegetable dishes to fill out the menu if you're welcoming an extra-large crowd. It wouldn't take much extra effort to fill a big pot with a mess of collard greens (with luck they've been kissed by frost by the last Thursday in November, which means they'll be good and sweet): Just simmer them on a back burner, with a smoked ham hock if that's how you roll, until they're very tender. Or roast a few halved Vidalia onions and top with buttered toasted bread crumbs.

One thing peculiar to holiday meals in the South are oysters, which are at their plumpest and sweetest this time of year. Do try the oyster stuffing here for a truly authentic southern Thanksgiving.

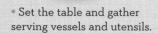

- Set the table and gather serving vessels and utensils.

- Chill wine.

6 HOURS IN ADVANCE

- Start roasting the turkey in one oven.

- Prepare the Herbed Oyster Stuffing and the Sourdough Stuffing with Sweet Potatoes and Cranberries just to the point where they're ready to go into the oven.

- Begin Alabama Spoon Bread: Mix wet and dry ingredients separately (see Tip); refrigerate wet ingredients.

- Set up coffee maker so it's ready for dessert time.

1 TO 2 HOURS IN ADVANCE

- Preheat the (second) oven to 350°F. Finish mixing spoon bread and put in oven. Put the two stuffings in the oven. Uncover yams and put in the oven.

- Make mashed potatoes.

LAST MINUTE

- Reheat green beans.

- Open a can of cranberry sauce.

- Carve turkey.

NO-BASTE, NO-BOTHER ROASTED TURKEY

INGREDIENTS

- ½ cup salted butter, softened
- 1 (12-pound) turkey completely thawed, all giblets removed
- 2 tablespoons salt
- 2 teaspoons ground black pepper
- 2 stalks celery, cut in lengths to fit turkey cavity
- 1 medium sweet onion (such as Vidalia) cut in half
- 1 large carrot
- 2 cups boiling water

THIS RECIPE IS FROM *GEORGIA COOKING IN AN OKLAHOMA KITCHEN: RECIPES FROM MY FAMILY TO YOURS*, BY TRISHA YEARWOOD.

1. Adjust oven racks so covered roasting pan fits easily inside oven. Preheat oven to 500°F.

2. Rub butter on outside of turkey and in cavity. A self-basting turkey will not require all the butter. Sprinkle salt and pepper on outside of turkey. Put celery, onion, and carrot in cavity. Place turkey, breast side up, in large roasting pan. Pour boiling water into pan. Cover with tight-fitting lid and put pan in preheated oven.

3. Start a timer when oven temperature returns to 500°F. Bake exactly 1 hour and turn off oven. Do not open oven door. Leave turkey in oven until oven cools; this may take 4 to 6 hours. Reserve pan juices and refrigerate turkey if it will not be served immediately after roasting.

EACH SERVING: About 432 calories, 64g protein, 0g carbohydrate, 18g total fat (7g saturated), 249mg cholesterol, 1,148mg sodium

HERBED OYSTER STUFFING

INGREDIENTS

- 1 **pound French country bread, cut into ½-inch cubes (12 cups)**
- 6 **stalks celery**
- 4 **large (2 to 3 ounces each) shallots**
- 4 **cloves garlic**
- 2 **tablespoons fresh thyme leaves**
- ½ **cup packed fresh flat-leaf parsley leaves**
- 3 **slices thick-cut bacon**
- 1 **cup shucked oysters**
- 4 **tablespoons (½ stick) butter or margarine, plus more for greasing pan**
- ¼ **teaspoon ground black pepper**
  low-sodium chicken broth (to add to oyster broth if necessary; optional)

JUST A CUP OF OYSTERS COMPLETELY TRANSFORMS THIS TRADITIONAL SOUTHERN STUFFING'S TASTE. TO AMP UP THEIR BRININESS WE MIX IN SLICES OF SMOKY, SALTY BACON.

1. Preheat oven to 350°F. In 18" by 12" jelly-roll pan, spread bread evenly. Bake 30 minutes or until golden brown and crisp, stirring once. Cool completely and transfer to large bowl.

2. Meanwhile, finely chop celery, shallots, garlic, thyme, and parsley separately. Cut bacon crosswise into ¼-inch pieces. Coarsely chop oysters, cover, and refrigerate until ready to use. With fine-mesh sieve, strain oyster liquid into liquid measuring cup (you should have 1 cup); cover and refrigerate until ready to use. Generously grease 3-quart shallow glass or ceramic baking dish with butter.

3. In 12-inch skillet, cook bacon over medium heat 8 minutes or until browned and crisp, stirring occasionally. With slotted spoon, transfer to bowl with bread. Drain all but 2 tablespoons fat from skillet.

4. To skillet, add celery and shallots. Cook over medium heat 5 minutes or until just tender, stirring occasionally. Transfer to bowl with bread. In same skillet over medium heat, melt margarine. Add garlic and thyme and cook 1 to 2 minutes or until fragrant and golden, stirring. Transfer to bowl with bread, along with parsley, oysters, oyster liquid, and pepper. Stir until well mixed.

5. Transfer stuffing to prepared baking dish and spread in even layer. Cover with foil and bake 30 minutes. Uncover and bake 20 minutes longer or until top is golden brown.

EACH SERVING: About 225 calories, 8g protein, 26g carbohydrate, 10g total fat (2g saturated), 27mg cholesterol, 420mg sodium

SOURDOUGH STUFFING WITH SWEET POTATOES & CRANBERRIES

⅓| SERVES 10

INGREDIENTS

- 4 tablespoons (½ stick) butter, plus more for greasing pan
- 1 large Vidalia onion, chopped
- 1 pound peeled sweet potatoes, cut into ½-inch cubes
- 2 tablespoons maple syrup
- 1 cup dried cranberries
- 2 tablespoons chopped fresh sage
- 1 teaspoon salt
- 1½ teaspoons ground black pepper
- 8 cups (½-inch cubes) sourdough bread
- 1¾ cups low-sodium chicken broth

CRANBERRIES ADD A SPLASH OF COLOR AND A WEALTH OF FLAVOR TO THIS DELECTABLE THANKSGIVING STUFFING.

1. Preheat oven to 350°F. Lightly butter 9" by 13" baking dish and set aside.

2. Melt 3 tablespoons butter in large Dutch oven over medium-high heat. Add onion and cook until soft, about 4 minutes.

3. Reduce heat to medium, add sweet potatoes, and cook until soft and onion is browned, about 20 minutes. Add maple syrup, cranberries, and 2 tablespoons water. Cook until cranberries plump, about 3 minutes. Add sage, salt, and pepper and cook 1 minute more.

4. Remove from heat and toss in bread and broth. Transfer to prepared dish, dot with remaining 1 tablespoon butter, and bake until heated through and top is golden, 30 to 40 minutes.

EACH SERVING: About 272 calories, 6g protein, 48g carbohydrate, 7g total fat (3g saturated), 12mg cholesterol, 596mg sodium

SOUTHERN-STYLE GREEN BEANS

INGREDIENTS

¾ pound salt-pork fatback

3 pounds fresh green beans

Salt and ground black pepper, to taste

THESE VERY TENDER, SLOW-SIMMERED GREEN BEANS ARE A MUST ON ANY SOUTHERN-STYLE THANKSGIVING MENU.

Cut three slits in fatback. In a medium saucepan over high heat, bring 2½ quarts water to a boil. Reduce heat to medium-low, add fatback, and simmer, covered, for 1 hour. Stir in beans and cook 40 to 45 minutes, until tender. Discard fatback. Season with salt and pepper.

EACH SERVING: About 73 calories, 3g protein, 13g carbohydrate, 2g total fat (1g saturated), 2mg cholesterol, 4mg sodium

ALABAMA SPOON BREAD WITH PUMPKIN & CHIVES

⇥ SERVES 8

INGREDIENTS

1½ cups buttermilk

1 cup solid-pack pumpkin (not pumpkin-pie mix)

4 large eggs, separated

3 tablespoons chopped fresh chives

4 tablespoons (½ stick) butter or margarine

1½ cups yellow cornmeal

1 tablespoon brown sugar

1 teaspoon baking soda

¾ teaspoon salt

⅛ teaspoon coarsely ground black pepper

A CROSS BETWEEN CORNBREAD AND A SOUFFLÉ, THIS PUDDING-LIKE SIDE DISH IS USUALLY SOFT ENOUGH TO EAT WITH A SPOON.

1. Preheat oven to 350°F. Lightly grease shallow 2½-quart ceramic baking dish. In medium bowl, with fork or wire whisk, mix buttermilk, pumpkin, egg yolks, and 2 tablespoons chives.

2. In 4-quart saucepan, heat butter and 1½ cups water to boiling over high heat. Remove from heat. In small bowl, whisk cornmeal, brown sugar, baking soda, salt, and pepper. Gradually whisk cornmeal mixture into hot liquid until blended. Then whisk in pumpkin mixture.

3. In small bowl, with electric mixer on high speed, beat egg whites just until stiff peaks form. Gently fold egg whites, one-third at a time, into cornmeal mixture until blended. Spoon batter into baking dish and sprinkle with remaining 1 tablespoon chives.

4. Place baking dish in roasting pan on oven rack. Pour boiling water into roasting pan until it reaches halfway up side of baking dish. Bake spoon bread 50 to 55 minutes until lightly browned and puffed and knife inserted 2 inches from center comes out clean.

EACH SERVING: About 220 calories, 7g protein, 27g carbohydrate, 9g total fat (2g saturated), 108mg cholesterol, 515mg sodium

> TIP Although this is not a do-ahead dish, you can ease the last-minute prep by combining the wet ingredients per step 1 (cover and refrigerate); then whisk together the dry ingredients per step 2, and set aside.

PRALINE CANDIED GARNET YAMS

⇥ SERVES 8

INGREDIENTS

- 5 pounds garnet yams or sweet potatoes, of equal size
- ½ cup (1 stick) cold unsalted butter, cut into 8 pieces
- ½ cup cane syrup
- 1 teaspoon kosher salt
- ¼ teaspoon freshly ground black pepper
- ¾ cup pecans, coarsely chopped
- ⅓ cup all-purpose flour
- ⅓ cup packed light brown sugar
- ½ teaspoon ground cinnamon

THESE TRADITIONAL CANDIED YAMS, WHICH WAFT SCENTS OF BUTTER, BROWN SUGAR, AND CINNAMON WHILE BAKING, COMPLETE THE THANKSGIVING DINNER MENU.

1. Preheat oven to 400°F. Place yams on baking sheet and roast 50 minutes or until they are just barely tender yet still hold their shape. Let cool completely. (Can be made up to 2 days ahead; refrigerate.)

2. Remove skins from yams and cut yams into ½-inch-thick slices. Butter a 2-quart baking dish with 1 tablespoon butter. Arrange yam slices in dish, slightly overlapping.

3. Heat syrup, salt, pepper, and 4 tablespoons butter in small saucepan over medium heat until butter melts; whisk to combine. Pour mixture over yams. (Cover and refrigerate if preparing in advance.)

4. Preheat oven to 375°F (or 350°F if baking straight from refrigerator). In small bowl, combine pecans, flour, sugar, and cinnamon; add remaining 3 tablespoons butter and rub in with fingers until mixture is evenly moistened and forms clumps; sprinkle over yams.

5. Bake 35 minutes or until praline topping is browned and yams are heated through.

EACH SERVING: About 441 calories, 4g protein, 66g carbohydrate, 16g total fat (7g saturated), 30mg cholesterol, 367mg sodium

CRACKED-PEPPER DINNER ROLLS

⊰| MAKES 16

INGREDIENTS

- 3⅓ cups all-purpose flour, plus more for kneading, if necessary
- 4 teaspoons (from 2 packets) quick-rise yeast
- 2 teaspoons sugar
- ¼ teaspoon salt
- 2 teaspoons freshly ground black pepper
- 2 large eggs (1 separated)
- 4 teaspoons butter, melted, plus more for pan

A HINT OF SPICY BLACK PEPPER ADDS A KICK TO THESE TRADITIONAL DINNER ROLLS.

1. In large bowl, combine 2⅔ cups flour, yeast, sugar, salt, and pepper.

2. In medium bowl, whisk together 1 egg and 1 egg white. Whisk in ⅔ cup warm water (120°F to 130°F) and melted butter. Using a wooden spoon, stir egg mixture into flour mixture until a soft dough forms.

3. Sprinkle ⅓ cup flour onto work surface. Transfer dough to surface. Sprinkle dough with remaining ⅓ cup flour and knead until smooth and elastic, about 5 minutes. (If sticky, add another 2 to 3 tablespoons flour.) Pat dough into a ball. Place in a large bowl, cover with a clean towel, and let rise, about 20 minutes.

4. Punch down dough. Divide into 16 equal portions, forming each into a ball (about 1¾ inches in diameter). Transfer balls to a buttered 16-muffin pan. Cover with lightly buttered plastic wrap and let dough rise until doubled in size, about 30 minutes.

5. Preheat oven to 350°F. In a small bowl, beat 1½ teaspoons water and remaining egg yolk. Brush tops of rolls with half the egg wash. Bake until golden brown and rolls sound hollow when tapped, 20 to 25 minutes. Brush tops with remaining egg wash. Return pan to oven and bake for 5 minutes more. Transfer rolls to wire rack to cool.

EACH SERVING: About 115 calories, 4g protein, 21g carbohydrate, 2g total fat (1g saturated), 26mg cholesterol, 119mg sodium

DILLY SNAP BEANS

⤙ MAKES 6 PINTS

INGREDIENTS

- 2 small chile peppers
- 12 sprigs fresh dill
- 12 cloves garlic, smashed
- 12 whole cloves
- ¼ cup dill seeds
- ¼ cup mustard seeds
- ¼ cup kosher salt
- 3 pounds green beans, ends trimmed to leave ½ inch headspace in jars
- 5 cups apple cider vinegar

CRISP, TANGY PICKLED GREEN BEANS MAKE A HEALTHY SNACK, A TANGY ADDITION TO SALADS OR SANDWICHES, OR A SURPRISING STIRRER FOR A SAVORY COCKTAIL.

1. In each of 6 sterilized pint-size canning jars, add 2 chile peppers, 2 dill sprigs, 2 garlic cloves, 2 whole cloves, 2 teaspoons dill seeds, 2 teaspoons mustard seeds, and 2 teaspoons salt. Tightly pack beans in jars.

2. In large saucepan over high heat, bring vinegar and 5 cups water to a boil. Pour hot liquid over beans, seal jars tightly, and refrigerate 2 weeks to allow flavors to develop. Beans will keep, refrigerated, up to 1 month.

EACH SERVING: About 38 calories, 2g protein, 8g carbohydrate, 0g total fat (0g saturated), 0mg cholesterol, 586mg sodium

PICKLES

MY MOM DIDN'T GROW UP IN THE SOUTH, but her family had one thing in common with southerners when it came to big holiday meals: the pickles. She always said you had to serve seven sweets (most in the form of pie) and seven sours (pickles and relishes). My aunt Kathy, in Virginia, would always serve Dilly Beans very much like the ones here, along with several other pickled vegetables, at her legendary Thanksgiving dinners. The tart, bright note pickles bring to the plate does wonders to cut through the heaviness of roast turkey, stuffing (or "dressing"), and mashed potatoes. For a fun, retro touch, round up a classic glass relish tray for serving your pickles.

SWEET POTATO PIE WITH BUTTERMILK ICE CREAM

SERVES 6

INGREDIENTS

2 medium sweet potatoes, peeled and chopped into ½-inch cubes

4 tablespoons (½ stick) unsalted butter, melted

2 tablespoons fresh lemon juice

½ teaspoon freshly grated nutmeg

½ teaspoon ground cinnamon

½ teaspoon kosher salt

3 large eggs, separated

½ cup sugar

2 tablespoons all-purpose flour

¾ cup buttermilk

One 9-Inch Baked Pie Shell (page 110); or a frozen ready-made crust, prebaked according to package instructions

Buttermilk Ice Cream (page 111), for serving

NO THANKSGIVING MEAL IS COMPLETE WITHOUT THE PERFECT SWEET POTATO PIE. LOOK NO FURTHER; YOU'VE FOUND IT!

1. Preheat oven to 375°F. Pour 1½ inches of water into a medium stockpot with a steamer basket and bring to a boil over medium-high heat. Add sweet potatoes, cover, and steam until fork-tender, about 20 minutes. Drain sweet potatoes, place in a large bowl, and let cool to room temperature. Mash them to a smooth puree with a fork or a potato masher (you should have 1¼ cups puree; discard any excess). Add butter, lemon juice, nutmeg, cinnamon, and salt, mixing after each addition.

2. In small bowl, beat egg yolks lightly with a whisk for about 30 seconds. Add sugar and beat until they're a creamy lemon-yellow color, about 1½ minutes. Add egg mixture to sweet potato mixture and stir until eggs are thoroughly incorporated and filling is a consistent bright-orange color. Add flour a little at a time, stirring after each addition, until thoroughly incorporated. Add buttermilk and stir to incorporate.

3. With clean, dry whisk and in separate bowl, whisk egg whites to soft peaks, about 1½ minutes. Gently fold egg whites into sweet potato–buttermilk mixture until thoroughly combined. Pour mixture into prepared pie shell and bake on middle rack of oven until the center is firm and set, 35 to 40 minutes.

4. Remove pie from oven and cool completely on a rack. Serve at room temperature with a scoop of ice cream on the side.

EACH SERVING: About 561 calories, 10g protein, 71g carbohydrate, 26g total fat (13g saturated), 140mg cholesterol, 615mg sodium

9-INCH BAKED PIE SHELL

INGREDIENTS

- 1⅓ cups all-purpose flour
- ¼ teaspoon salt
- 5 tablespoons cold butter or margarine, cut up
- 3 tablespoons vegetable shortening
- 5 tablespoons ice water

1. In food processor with knife blade attached, blend flour and salt. Add butter and shortening and pulse until mixture resembles coarse crumbs. Sprinkle in ice water, 1 tablespoon at a time, pulsing after each addition, until large moist crumbs just begin to form.

2. Shape dough into disk; wrap in plastic wrap and refrigerate 30 minutes or overnight. (If chilled overnight, let dough stand 30 minutes at room temperature before rolling.)

3. Preheat oven to 425°F. On lightly floured surface, with floured rolling pin, roll dough into 12-inch round. Ease dough round into 9-inch glass or ceramic pie plate. Gently press dough against bottom and up sides of plate without stretching. Trim dough edge, leaving 1-inch overhang. Fold overhang under; pinch to form stand-up edge, then make decorative edge. Freeze pie shell 15 minutes.

4. Line pie shell with foil or parchment and fill with pie weights, dried beans, or uncooked rice. Bake 10 to 12 minutes, until beginning to set. Remove foil with weights and bake 13 to 15 minutes longer, until golden. If shell puffs up during baking, gently press it down with back of spoon. Cool on wire rack until ready to fill.

TIP To make the crust by hand: In step 1, combine flour and salt in a large bowl, and with a pastry blender or two knives used scissors-fashion, cut in butter and shortening until mixture resembles coarse crumbs. Add ice water, mixing lightly with a fork after each addition, until dough is just moist enough to hold together. Continue with recipe.

BUTTERMILK ICE CREAM

INGREDIENTS

4 large egg yolks
½ cup sugar
2 cups heavy cream
1½ cups cold buttermilk

1. Whisk egg yolks lightly in medium bowl. Add sugar and beat until mixture is a milky lemon-yellow color, about 1 minute.

2. Heat cream and 1 cup buttermilk in small saucepan over medium-low heat, while stirring, until a thermometer reads 150°F, 6 to 8 minutes (milk should not boil).

3. Pour cream mixture in a thin stream into egg mixture, whisking continually until incorporated. Transfer to clean container and refrigerate until very cold, 4 hours or up to overnight.

4. Add remaining ½ cup buttermilk and stir to incorporate. Freeze custard in an ice-cream maker according to manufacturer's instructions. Transfer to airtight container, cover surface with plastic wrap, and seal lid. Freeze at least 2 hours. Let sit for 10 minutes before serving.

NOTE: This recipe contains raw egg and should not be consumed by pregnant women, infants, the ill, or the elderly.

EACH SERVING: About 401 calories, 6g protein, 23g carbohydrate, 33g total fat (20g saturated), 249mg cholesterol, 103mg sodium

OLD-FASHIONED PECAN PIE

INGREDIENTS

- ¾ cup dark corn syrup
- ½ cup dark brown sugar
- 3 tablespoons butter or margarine, melted
- 1 teaspoon vanilla extract
  Pinch salt
- 3 large eggs
- 1½ cups pecan halves, toasted
  9-Inch Baked Pie Shell (page 110); or a frozen ready-made crust, prebaked according to package instructions

HOMEMADE CRUST AND COPIOUS AMOUNTS OF DARK CORN SYRUP GIVE THIS TRADITIONAL PECAN PIE A LEG UP ON THE COMPETITION.

1. Prepare 9-Inch Baked Pie Shell as recipe directs. Cool pie shell on wire rack at least 10 minutes. Reset oven temperature to 350°F.

2. In large bowl, with wire whisk, mix corn syrup, brown sugar, butter, vanilla, salt, and eggs until blended. With spoon, stir in pecans.

3. Pour filling into pie shell. Bake 43 to 45 minutes, until filling is set around edge but center jiggles slightly. Cool on wire rack at least 3 hours for easier slicing. Refrigerate leftovers up to 1 week.

EACH SERVING: About 410 calories, 5g protein, 41g carbohydrate, 27g total fat (9g saturated), 90mg cholesterol, 220mg sodium

TIP For a grown-up version, add 2 tablespoons bourbon and ¼ teaspoon freshly grated nutmeg to egg mixture in step 2.

HUMMINGBIRD CAKE

SERVES 12

INGREDIENTS

CAKE

Butter, for greasing pans

3 cups all-purpose flour, unsifted

2 cups granulated sugar

1 teaspoon baking soda

1 teaspoon ground cinnamon

½ teaspoon salt

3 large eggs

¾ cup vegetable oil

1¾ cups ripe bananas, mashed (about 2)

1 can (18 ounces) crushed pineapple, with juice

1 cup chopped pecans

2 teaspoons vanilla extract

CREAM CHEESE FROSTING

1 package (8 ounces) cream cheese, softened

1 stick (½ cup) butter, softened

1 teaspoon vanilla extract

1 box (1 pound) confectioners' sugar, sifted

¾ cup roughly chopped pecans

THIS SOUTHERN CLASSIC TAKES ITS NAME FROM THE FACT THAT IT TASTES SO GOOD, YOU'LL "HUM" WHEN YOU EAT IT. UNLIKE MOST CAKE BATTERS, THIS ONE IS MADE IN A SINGLE BOWL AND MIXED WITH JUST A WOODEN SPOON.

1. Prepare cake: Preheat oven to 350°F. Butter and flour three 9-inch round cake pans. In large bowl, combine flour, sugar, baking soda, cinnamon, and salt. Add eggs and vegetable oil, stirring until dry ingredients are moistened; do not beat. Stir in bananas, pineapple with juice, pecans, and vanilla.

2. Divide batter evenly among cake pans. Bake until cake tester inserted into center of cake layer comes out clean, 25 to 30 minutes. Let cakes cool in pans 10 minutes, then invert onto wire racks to cool completely.

3. Prepare cream cheese frosting: In medium bowl with electric mixer on medium speed, beat cream cheese, butter, and vanilla until smooth. Reduce speed to low and slowly add confectioners' sugar until frosting thickens.

4. Place one cake layer on a cake plate. Cover top with frosting; repeat with remaining two layers. Cover sides of cake with remaining frosting. Sprinkle pecans over top.

EACH SERVING: About 812 calories, 8g protein, 115g carbohydrate, 39g total fat (13g saturated), 93mg cholesterol, 321mg sodium

FIRESIDE DRINKS

Shrimp Mousse

Pimento Cheese Log

Fried Tomatillos with
Creamy Cumin Dip

Mini Bread Puddings

Crackers for Cheese Log
& Mousse

Cranberry Julep

Mulled cider or
Hot Buttered Bourbon
or both!

TIMELINE

UP TO 1 WEEK IN ADVANCE

• Make cranberry syrup
(step 1 of Cranberry Juleps).

• Crush ice for juleps and
keep in heavy-duty plastic
bag or other airtight container
in the freezer.

UP TO 3 DAYS IN ADVANCE

• Make Pimento Cheese Log.

UP TO 1 DAY AND AT LEAST 4 HOURS IN ADVANCE

• Make Shrimp Mousse.

• Make cumin dip for Fried
Tomatillos with Creamy
Cumin Dip (step 1).

• Toast bread and crush
peppermints for Mini Bread

Puddings; set aside at room
temperature.

UP TO 4 HOURS IN ADVANCE

• Continue juleps through
step 2: Make fresh cranberry
garnishes and mix syrup and
bourbon; cover and refrigerate. Chill glasses.

I N THE RUN-UP TO THE BUSY HOLIDAY SEASON, it's always a good idea to make time for a celebration that has nothing to do with wrapping presents, overland travel, and family obligations. Don't let the lack of an actual fireplace keep you from inviting a few friends over for drinks and old-school southern hors d'oeuvres on a chill autumn evening. Get creative! Arrange some comfortable chairs and side tables around a makeshift hearth: stuff some string lights inside a big lantern, or group a bunch of large candles on a coffee table. Or take the party outside and build a wood fire in a brazier; offer lap blankets to your guests for extra warmth as the darkness falls.

This menu features two traditional spreads to go with crackers or cut vegetables: pimento cheese and a fun molded shrimp mousse. Individual warm bread puddings satisfy a sweet tooth. Appetizers from other chapters would be welcome here if you need to bulk up the menu—for example, the spiced pecans on page 40 or the deviled eggs on page 142.

• Make mulled cider: Simmer apple cider, whole spices, and brown sugar to taste. Keep warm in a slow cooker if you'd like, or reheat just before serving. Cut pats of butter and keep in the refrigerator for hot buttered Bourbon, if you'd like.

UP TO 2 HOURS IN ADVANCE

• Make bread puddings.

• Whip cream for bread puddings.

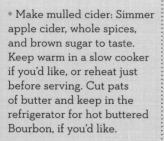

LAST 30 MINUTES

• Set out crackers, cheese log, and shrimp mousse.

• Make fried tomatillos.

• Set out crushed ice and chilled glasses, along with chilled cranberry Bourbon

mixture and mint sprigs for guests to help themselves.

• Boil water and set out butter and bottle of Bourbon, and mugs for hot buttered Bourbon. Reheat mulled cider if necessary and ladle into mugs.

SHRIMP MOUSSE

INGREDIENTS

- 1 envelope (¼ ounce) unflavored gelatin
- 1 can (10¾ ounces) condensed tomato soup
- 8 ounces cream cheese
- ½ cup finely chopped celery
- ½ cup finely chopped green onion
- ½ cup finely chopped green bell pepper
- 1 cup mayonnaise
- 2 teaspoons fresh lemon juice
- ¼ teaspoon Cajun seasoning
- ¼ teaspoon Worcestershire sauce
- ¼ teaspoon Tabasco sauce
- ⅛ teaspoon ground black pepper
- ¾ pound cooked shrimp, shelled, deveined, and chopped

THIS TRADITIONAL GULF COAST APPETIZER CAN BE MADE UP TO TWO DAYS IN ADVANCE. COOKED LOBSTER OR CRABMEAT MAKES AN EXCELLENT SUBSTITUTE FOR THE SHRIMP.

1. In a saucepan, sprinkle gelatin into ¼ cup water. Stir to dissolve and gently heat until clear. Add soup and cream cheese and cook over low heat, stirring until mixture is smooth. Remove from heat and fold in remaining ingredients.

2. Pour into a lightly greased 6-cup mold. Cover and chill until set, about 4 hours. Unmold and serve with crackers.

EACH SERVING: About 374 calories, 13g protein, 8g carbohydrate, 33g total fat (8g saturated), 130mg cholesterol, 623mg sodium

PIMENTO CHEESE LOG

⊰ MAKES 2 LOGS

INGREDIENTS

- 3 tablespoons roasted salted almonds
- ¼ cup packed fresh flat-leaf parsley leaves
- 2 jarred piquillo peppers, patted dry
- 8 ounces reduced-fat cream cheese, such as Neufchâtel
- 4 ounces goat cheese
- ½ teaspoon ground coriander
- ⅛ teaspoon cayenne (ground red pepper)
- 1 teaspoon coarsely ground pink peppercorns or ½ teaspoon freshly ground black pepper

YOUR GUESTS WILL LOVE THIS PARTY FAVORITE—THE FRESH GREEN HERB AND PINK PEPPER COATING DELIVERS A HEARTY DOSE OF HOLIDAY CHEER. SERVE WITH CELERY STICKS OR CRACKERS.

1. In food processor, pulse almonds until finely chopped. Transfer to large sheet of plastic wrap. Pulse parsley until finely chopped; transfer to plastic wrap with almonds. Wipe bowl.

2. In cleaned food processor, pulse piquillo peppers until finely chopped. Add cheeses, coriander, and cayenne and pulse, occasionally scraping bowl. Transfer mixture to clean sheet of plastic wrap and form into 12-inch-long log.

3. Add pink peppercorns to parsley mixture; mix well. Spread in 12" by 5" rectangle. Using plastic wrap, place cheese log on parsley mixture. Roll and gently press into parsley mixture. Wrap tightly in the plastic wrap. Refrigerate until firm, about 3 hours. Log can be refrigerated up to 3 days. To serve, cut log crosswise to form two smaller logs.

EACH SERVING: About 65 calories, 3g protein, 1g carbohydrate, 6g total fat (3g saturated), 14mg cholesterol, 90mg sodium

PIMENTO CHEESE

THE SOUTH'S BELOVED PIMENTO CHEESE is having a moment on fancy restaurant menus all over the country. Everyone has his or her own preferred recipe, and a discussion of minor variations can quickly become a heated debate. A purist would use only diced jarred pimentos, freshly shredded cheddar cheese, and mayonnaise (preferably Duke's, which is less sweet than other major brands). And now here's where things can go off the rails. Some people (myself included) will use part mayo and part cream cheese, a ton of fresh-roasted bell peppers, fresh lemon juice, ground cayenne, a dash of vinegar-based hot sauce, and a bit of grated sweet Vidalia onion.

FRIED TOMATILLOS WITH CREAMY CUMIN DIP

INGREDIENTS

½ cup sour cream

⅓ cup mayonnaise

1 tablespoon hot sauce

1¼ teaspoons ground cumin

1 teaspoon fresh lime juice

¼ teaspoon ground coriander

8 large tomatillos, husked and rinsed

3 large eggs

2 cups plain dried breadcrumbs

1 cup all-purpose flour

2 teaspoons salt

1 cup canola oil

SIMILAR TO THE CLASSIC FAVORITE FRIED GREEN TOMATOES, THESE JUICY BITES ARE KICKED UP A NOTCH WITH A CUMIN-LACED DIP.

1. In medium bowl, combine sour cream, mayonnaise, hot sauce, ¼ teaspoon cumin, lime juice, and coriander. Refrigerate dip until ready to serve.

2. Cut tomatillos into ¼-inch-thick slices and set aside. In shallow small bowl, beat eggs. In shallow medium bowl, combine bread-crumbs, flour, salt, and remaining 1 teaspoon cumin.

3. In skillet over medium-high heat, heat canola oil. Working in batches, dip tomatillo slices in egg, then in breading; shake off excess. Repeat. Fry the slices until deep golden brown, 2 to 4 minutes per side. Drain on paper towel–lined plate. Serve immediately with dip.

EACH SERVING: About 520 calories, 11g protein, 47g carbohydrate, 32g total fat (5g saturated), 109mg cholesterol, 1,220mg sodium

MINI BREAD PUDDINGS

INGREDIENTS

- 12 slices white bread
- 1⅓ cups semisweet chocolate chips
- 10 large eggs
- 1 cup sugar
- 1 teaspoon vanilla extract
- ¼ teaspoon salt
- 1½ cups whole milk
- 1½ cups heavy cream
   Whipped cream (optional)
   Crushed peppermints (optional)

TOPPED WITH WHIPPED CREAM AND CRUSHED PEPPER-MINTS, THESE SINGLE-SERVING BREAD PUDDINGS MAKE PERFECT DESSERTS FOR A BUFFET-STYLE HOLIDAY PARTY.

1. Preheat oven to 350°F. Toast bread on two baking sheets, flipping after 7 minutes, until slices are dry but not brown, about 15 minutes. Cool completely on pans.

2. Meanwhile, line 20 cups in two standard-size muffin tins with paper liners. Cut cooled toast into ½-inch cubes and divide among muffin cups, along with chocolate chips. Gently shake tins to distribute chips evenly; set aside.

3. In a large bowl, whisk eggs, sugar, vanilla, and salt until sugar is dissolved. Add milk and cream and continue whisking until smooth. Pour custard evenly over bread cubes and chocolate chips in muffin cups. Let stand until bread absorbs custard, about 20 minutes.

4. Place muffin tins on pans with 1-inch sides. Pour water into pans, creating a bath around muffin tins. Bake until custard sets and tops are golden, 45 to 50 minutes. Cool in muffin tins on a wire rack.

EACH SERVING: About 241 calories, 6g protein, 26g carbohydrate, 14g total fat (8g saturated), 120mg cholesterol, 159mg sodium

CRANBERRY JULEPS

INGREDIENTS

- ¾ cup sugar
- 2 strips (each 3 inches long) fresh orange peel, removed with vegetable peeler
- 1 cup fresh cranberries, plus additional for garnish
- 1 cup Kentucky bourbon
- 8 sprigs fresh mint

SIMPLE SYRUP INFUSED WITH CRANBERRY AND ORANGE PEEL GIVES THIS CLASSIC SOUTHERN COCKTAIL A SEASONAL TWIST.

1. In 2-quart saucepan, heat 1 cup water, sugar, and orange peel to boiling over high heat. Add cranberries and cook 2 to 3 minutes, until cranberries pop and split but still hold their shape. Remove from heat and cool to room temperature. Refrigerate until cold. (Syrup and cranberries can be refrigerated up to 1 week.)

2. When ready to serve, strain cranberry syrup through sieve set over 1-quart liquid measure; discard solids. Spear 3 raw cranberries on each of eight toothpicks. Stir bourbon into syrup.

3. Fill eight glasses with crushed ice. Divide bourbon mixture among glasses. Garnish with cranberry spears and mint.

EACH SERVING: About 150 calories, 0g protein, 23g carbohydrate, 0g total fat, 0mg cholesterol, 0mg sodium

WINTER

COZYING UP

I HATE TO BREAK IT TO THOSE who might believe that in the South it never gets cold, it never snows, and the dark never starts to feel oppressive in winter, but it does. **A Festive Christmas** might fall on a day when you wouldn't hesitate to go out barefoot, and there are times in March when you could easily hike down to the river in shirtsleeves and see the earliest daffodils in the woods. But there are also freak, paralyzing snowstorms that keep you holed up in the house for days at a time; there's chilling rain, which can be even more demoralizing than snow; and there are nights in Florida, of all places, so bone-cold you wish you hadn't given away your winter coat when you moved there from up north.

Dark days call for homey food and as many impromptu get-togethers as possible. There's no better excuse for a **Midwinter Potluck** with neighbors (and winter's when a big Dutch oven or slow cooker of chili—the preeminent potluck dish—will surely be most welcome). Brighten the table with fresh citrus and hearty greens, and comfort guests with creamy winter squash and potatoes every which way. And don't forget to throw down a feast for a **Mardi Gras Bash**.

WHAT'S IN SEASON

Brussels sprouts
Grapefruit
Hardy greens
Oranges
Potatoes
Sweet potatoes
Winter squash

11

A FESTIVE CHRISTMAS

Breakfast Strata

Coffee or tea, orange juice

Holiday Oyster Stew

Pecan-Baked Ham

Sweet Potato Biscuits

Roasted Brussels sprouts

Simple green salad
or steamed green beans

Peppermint Divinity

Buttermilk Custard
with Navel Oranges in
Red Wine Syrup

Red wine

TIMELINE

BREAKFAST TIMELINE

CHRISTMAS EVE

- Prepare Breakfast Strata through step 4.

CHRISTMAS MORNING

- Make coffee, squeeze OJ.
- Bake and enjoy the strata.

DINNER TIMELINE

UP TO 2 WEEKS IN ADVANCE

- Make Peppermint Divinity; store in an airtight container at room temperature.

1 DAY IN ADVANCE

- Make Sweet Potato Biscuits; keep in an airtight container at room temperature.

- Prepare buttermilk custard; cover glasses with plastic wrap and refrigerate. Prepare red wine syrup; cover and

refrigerate. Segment oranges; cover and refrigerate.

- Make spice-pecan mix for Pecan-Baked Ham.

- If making salad, wash and spin dry salad greens; wrap in paper towels, put in a plastic bag, and refrigerate.

I'VE NEVER GOTTEN A DEFINITIVE ANSWER to the question of whether Christmas dinner in the South traditionally occurs on December 24 or 25, but this special menu will do well on any winter evening. Ham is a must, of course, as it is all over the country, but to make this meal truly southern you must also have buttery, briny oyster stew. Look for tubs of shucked oysters on ice at your fishmonger, or use good-quality jarred ones in a pinch.

I've also included a recipe for a savory layered casserole that you can make the night before, refrigerate, and bake in the morning for an easy, satisfying, homey breakfast. It's not quite the one my mom always makes for Christmas Day (she used to serve it with Orange Julius–style milkshakes, believe it or not!), but it's close enough.

- Trim and halve Brussels sprouts, toss with oil and chopped garlic, cover, and refrigerate.

- Make simple vinaigrette for green salad and refrigerate.

- Set the table with soup plates and dinner plates.

2 HOURS IN ADVANCE

- Bake ham.

- Preheat baking sheet in oven while ham bakes, spread Brussels sprouts on baking sheet, season with salt and pepper, and roast until tender and golden, about 35 minutes at 375°F.

- Make Holiday Oyster Stew.

- Pull vinaigrette from fridge to come to room temperature and whisk or shake to recombine.

LAST 30 MINUTES

- Toss greens with vinaigrette, or steam green beans and top with butter if desired.

- Assemble custards.

- Slice ham.

BREAKFAST STRATA

INGREDIENTS

- ¼ cup (½ stick) unsalted butter, softened
- 8 ounces (about 8 slices) thick-sliced smoked bacon, cut crosswise into ½-inch-wide strips
- 12 ounces large button mushrooms, sliced
- 1 cup chopped onion
- 2 teaspoons chopped fresh sage leaves
- 1 package (10 ounces) frozen chopped spinach, thawed and squeezed dry
- 8 slices (¾-inch-thick) brioche, challah, or potato bread
- 4 plum tomatoes, sliced
- 6 large eggs
- 3 cups milk
- ¾ cup grated Parmesan cheese
- ½ teaspoon ground black pepper
- 6 ounces Gruyère cheese, shredded or cut into small dice
- Chopped fresh parsley

START OFF CHRISTMAS MORNING IN A VERY SPECIAL WAY WITH THIS YUMMY BACON AND VEGGIE STRATA.

1. With 1 tablespoon butter, generously grease a large, shallow 2½- to 3-quart baking dish or casserole.

2. Cook bacon in skillet over medium heat until crisp. Remove bacon to drain on paper towel, leaving 2 tablespoons bacon drippings in skillet. To skillet, add mushrooms, onion, and sage; sauté over medium heat 8 to 10 minutes, until browned and mushrooms have released much of their liquid. Spread mixture over bottom of prepared baking dish; scatter spinach over top.

3. Spread remaining 3 tablespoons butter over one side of bread slices and arrange, buttered side up and overlapping, on top of spinach. Arrange 3 tomato slices on buttered side of each bread slice.

4. In large bowl with wire whisk, beat eggs, milk, ½ cup Parmesan, and pepper until well blended. Slowly pour egg mixture over bread slices; press bread down to absorb egg mixture, spooning egg mixture over any uncoated bread. Scatter Gruyère and remaining ¼ cup Parmesan over top. Cover strata and refrigerate overnight.

5. Bring strata to room temperature. Preheat oven to 350°F. Bake, uncovered, 30 minutes; loosely cover with foil to prevent overbrowning. Bake 25 minutes or until golden on top and a knife inserted in center comes out clean. Let stand 20 minutes before serving. Sprinkle with parsley.

EACH SERVING: About 605 calories, 33g protein, 34g carbohydrate, 37g total fat (21g saturated), 299mg cholesterol, 925mg sodium

YOUR OWN HOLIDAY TRADITIONS

I'M NOT INCLINED TO RIGIDLY ESTABLISH OR FOLLOW TRADITIONS for my family, but I've found that if you can't be in the same place every Christmas or Passover, say, or if you can't spend the holidays with the same people every year, you can still maintain some sense of continuity through the foods you cook and eat to celebrate. If we can't get to New York to visit my husband's family at Christmastime we can still seek out (or make) the best bagels and lox wherever we are, and make buttered mushrooms and Yorkshire pudding. If we can't get to my parents' house in December I can re-create at least a small part of the experience by making *springerle* and *fatig* cookies. Maybe some of the recipes in this section will eventually become a touchstone for your family in a similar way, bringing people together across great distances.

HOLIDAY OYSTER STEW

INGREDIENTS

- 3 tablespoons unsalted butter
- 2 shallots, minced
- 1 medium yellow onion, minced
- ½ cup minced celery
- 1 quart half-and-half
- 1 quart milk
- ¼ teaspoon cayenne (ground red pepper)
- 1 teaspoon salt
- 1 teaspoon cracked black pepper
- 2 pints fresh, raw, shucked oysters, liquor reserved
- 2 tablespoons slivered fresh basil leaves (optional)

THIS RICH, CREAMY OYSTER STEW IS BEST ON A COLD WINTER'S DAY. TO CRACK BLACK PEPPERCORNS, PUT SOME ON A CUTTING BOARD AND PRESS DOWN ON THEM WITH THE FLAT SIDE OF A KNIFE OR THE BOTTOM OF A HEAVY PAN.

Melt butter in soup pot over medium heat. Sauté shallots, onion, and celery until soft, about 5 minutes. Stir in half-and-half, milk, cayenne, salt, and pepper. Heat to just under a boil. Add oysters and their liquor. Simmer just until the oysters begin to curl on the edges, about 5 minutes. Ladle into soup bowls and sprinkle with basil, if desired.

EACH SERVING: About 367 calories, 17g protein, 18g carbohydrate, 25g total fat (14g saturated), 138mg cholesterol, 645mg sodium

PECAN-BAKED HAM

⊰| SERVES 12

INGREDIENTS

- 1 cup brown sugar
- ¼ cup finely chopped pecans
- 2 tablespoons unsalted butter, softened
- 1 tablespoon Chinese five-spice powder
- 1 (5-pound) good-quality cooked ham
- 2 medium onions, chopped

WITH JUST A FEW INGREDIENTS, THIS FESTIVE BAKED HAM IS THE PERFECT CENTERPIECE FOR A HOLIDAY TABLE.

1. Preheat oven to 350°F. In small bowl, mix brown sugar, pecans, butter, and five-spice powder to create a fine, crumbly mixture. Using your hands, rub mixture onto ham.

2. In bottom of heavy roasting pan, scatter onions; add 2 cups water. Place ham atop bed of onions and roast until glaze is glistening and deep brown, 1 hour 40 minutes to 2 hours, checking occasionally to make sure water hasn't evaporated (add ¼ to ½ cup more, as needed).

3. Slice ham and top with pan juices, including onions. If sauce is too thin, pour liquid into medium saucepan over medium-high heat and reduce until desired consistency is achieved.

EACH SERVING: About 405 calories, 32g protein, 27g carbohydrate, 17g total fat (7g saturated), 106mg cholesterol, 2,571mg sodium

SWEET POTATO BISCUITS

INGREDIENTS

- 2½ cups all-purpose flour
- 2 tablespoons baking powder
- ⅛ teaspoon allspice
- ⅛ teaspoon ground cloves
- ½ teaspoon salt
- ¼ cup packed light brown sugar
- 4 tablespoons (½ stick) unsalted butter, chilled
- ¼ cup shortening, chilled
- 1½ cups mashed cooked sweet potatoes
- 2 tablespoons milk

THESE DELIGHTFUL BISCUITS COMPLEMENT ANY HOMEMADE MEAL, BRINGING A SENSE OF WARMTH AND SWEETNESS TO THE TABLE.

1. Preheat oven to 425°F. Sift flour, baking powder, allspice, cloves, and salt in a large bowl. Use the tips of your fingers to blend in brown sugar.

2. Cut in butter and shortening with a pastry cutter or pulse in food processor until mixture resembles coarse, crumbly meal. Stir in sweet potatoes and knead until the dough just holds together.

3. Turn dough onto a lightly floured surface. Knead gently for 1 minute, adding a little flour as necessary to incorporate all the ingredients.

4. Pat dough into a ½-inch-thick circle and let rest, covered with a clean towel, 10 to 15 minutes.

5. Cut out biscuits with a 2-inch round cutter dipped in flour. Gather the scraps, pat out again, and cut into biscuits. Arrange them about ¾ inch apart on ungreased baking sheet and brush tops with milk. Bake until golden brown, 10 to 12 minutes. Cool on a rack.

EACH SERVING: About 134 calories, 2g protein, 19g carbohydrate, 6g total fat (2g saturated), 7mg cholesterol, 240mg sodium

PEPPERMINT DIVINITY

INGREDIENTS

4 cups sugar

1 cup light corn syrup

3 large egg whites

1½ teaspoons peppermint extract

6 drops red food coloring

THOUGH IT'S OFTEN MADE WITH CHOPPED NUTS, OUR VERSION OF THIS CLASSIC CHRISTMASTIME NOUGAT IS SMOOTH, CREAMY, AND SWEETLY PEPPERMINT. HAVE EVERYTHING READY BEFORE YOU START, AS ONCE THE CANDY REACHES TEMPERATURE, IT WILL IMMEDIATELY BEGIN TO HARDEN.

1. Oil 9-inch square pan and a spoon and set aside. Combine sugar and corn syrup in medium saucepan with ¾ cup water and cook over medium heat until mixture reaches 260°F on a candy thermometer, about 20 minutes.

2. In large bowl using an electric mixer, beat egg whites on medium-high speed until stiff peaks form. Reduce speed to medium and slowly pour sugar mixture into egg whites. Add peppermint and continue to beat until mixture is very thick and fluffy, about 12 minutes.

3. Immediately transfer to prepared pan and smooth using back of oiled spoon. Dot divinity surface with red food coloring and drag a skewer through to create a marbled effect. Let stand at room temperature until firm, about 2 hours. Slice into 1-inch squares.

NOTE: **For a simple variation, drop dollops of divinity batter onto an oiled baking sheet, then top with chocolate kisses.**

EACH SERVING (1 PIECE): About 114 calories, 0g protein, 29g carbohydrate, 0g total fat (0g saturated), 0mg cholesterol, 10mg sodium

BUTTERMILK CUSTARD WITH NAVEL ORANGES IN RED WINE SYRUP

INGREDIENTS

- 1 envelope (¼ ounce) powdered gelatin
- 3 cups cold buttermilk
- 1 cup heavy cream
- 3 cups plus 2 tablespoons sugar
- Kosher salt
- 1 bottle (750 ml) light red wine, such as Pinot Noir or claret
- 7 whole black peppercorns
- 2 navel oranges, peeled, segmented, and cut into bite-size pieces; reserve peel of 1 orange
- 2 red navel oranges, peeled, segmented, and cut into bite-size pieces

RED WINE, SUGAR, AND SEASONINGS BECOME A SWEET JEWEL-TONED SYRUP, WHICH OFFSETS THE TANGY CUSTARD IN THIS ELEGANT DESSERT FROM STEVEN SATTERFIELD.

1. Fill a double boiler with water and set over low heat, bringing water to a simmer. Meanwhile, in small bowl, sprinkle gelatin over buttermilk and allow to soften and expand, about 1 minute. Pour gelatin-buttermilk mixture into top of double boiler and heat, stirring constantly, until gelatin is completely dissolved, about 2 minutes, making sure liquid does not boil. Remove from heat and set aside.

2. In medium saucepan over medium-high heat, bring cream and 1 cup plus 2 tablespoons sugar to a boil. Remove from heat and add to gelatin-buttermilk mixture. Stir to combine, then pour mixture through a fine-mesh sieve into container with pouring spout. Season with salt. Divide custard among 6-ounce glasses and refrigerate until chilled and set, about 2 hours.

3. Meanwhile, in large saucepan, combine wine, remaining 2 cups sugar, peppercorns, orange peel, and 1 teaspoon salt and bring to a boil. Lower heat and simmer, uncovered, until mixture is reduced by one-third, 20 to 30 minutes. Remove from heat and let cool.

4. Divide orange segments over custards in glasses, then top fruit with 3 to 4 tablespoons red wine syrup and serve immediately. Any extra syrup can be stored in an airtight container in the refrigerator for up to 6 months.

EACH SERVING: About 456 calories, 6g protein, 76g carbohydrate, 10g total fat (7g saturated), 36mg cholesterol, 329mg sodium

MIDWINTER POTLUCK

Deviled Eggs
with Old Bay Shrimp

Texas-Style Chili

Sweet Corn Pudding

Self-Serve Hot-Chocolate Bar

TIMELINE

1 DAY IN ADVANCE

- Hard-cook eggs; cover and refrigerate.

4 HOURS IN ADVANCE

- Make Deviled Eggs with Old Bay Shrimp through step 2. Refrigerate.

- Set out hot chocolate fixings and mugs, plus napkins, bowls, and spoons for chili.

AFTER NEW YEAR'S EVE, the collective mood can either nosedive at the prospect of several more months of gray before the first blooms of spring or breathe a sigh of relief that the stress of the holiday season is over. In either case, a casual, easygoing potluck dinner is just the thing.

Prepare this simple menu and ask your guests to bring a few complementary side dishes. The chili can be simmering, the deviled eggs in the fridge, and the corn pudding coming out of the oven as guests arrive. To add to the atmosphere, set up a hot chocolate bar with creative fixings everyone will enjoy.

Potlucks sometimes get a bad rap because as meals they can be a bit scattershot—easily transportable but often composed of random dishes that don't always go together. As the host, make sure you have a basic selection of foods that could serve as a meal all ready to go when guests arrive. As a potluck guest, try to avoid bringing foods that need more than a quick reheat or that will take up fridge space. Keep it simple. To the party menu outlined here, you could bring the Collards with Pickled Red Onions, a jar of Quick-Pickled Bourbon Jalapeños, a batch of Jumbo Pecan-Date Oatmeal Cookies, or some of the garnishes for the hot chocolate bar.

2 HOURS IN ADVANCE

- Make Texas-Style Chili. If you prefer, make it earlier in the day and transfer to a slow cooker to keep warm.

- Make Sweet Corn Pudding, putting it in the oven about 40 minutes before serving.

LAST 30 MINUTES

- Set out chopped onions for chili.

- Slice and set out cornbread.

- Make white and classic hot chocolates, put in thermoses or hot drink dispensers.

- Garnish deviled eggs.

DEVILED EGGS WITH OLD BAY SHRIMP

INGREDIENTS

- 24 rock or bay shrimp, cooked and peeled
- 1 cup white wine vinegar
- 12 hard-boiled eggs, halved lengthwise, whites reserved
- ½ cup mayonnaise
- 2 tablespoons dill pickle juice
- 1 teaspoon Old Bay seasoning, plus more for garnish
- ½ teaspoon salt
- 24 sprigs fresh dill

THESE CREAMY DEVILED EGGS TOPPED WITH OLD BAY SEASONING AND PICKLED SHRIMP ARE EASY TO MAKE AND SURE TO IMPRESS.

1. In large bowl, combine shrimp and vinegar; refrigerate for 30 minutes. Meanwhile, in food processor, blend hard-boiled egg yolks, mayonnaise, pickle juice, Old Bay seasoning, and salt until smooth.

2. Drain shrimp and set aside. Distribute filling among reserved egg-white halves and sprinkle each with a pinch of Old Bay seasoning.

3. Top each deviled egg with a pickled shrimp and a sprig of dill. Serve immediately.

EACH SERVING: About 76 calories, 4g protein, 1g carbohydrate, 6g total fat (1g saturated), 103mg cholesterol, 155mg sodium

TEXAS-STYLE CHILI

INGREDIENTS

3½ pounds beef for stew

¼ cup vegetable oil

2 medium onions, chopped

3 medium green peppers, chopped

4 cloves garlic, crushed

2 cans (28 ounces each) tomatoes with liquid

1 can (12 ounces) tomato paste

⅓ cup chili powder

¼ cup sugar

2 teaspoons salt

2 teaspoons dried oregano leaves

¾ teaspoon cracked black pepper

A POT OF THIS CHILI SIMMERING ON THE RANGE BRINGS CHILDREN IN FROM THE COLD MIGHTY QUICKLY. LITTLE CHUNKS OF TENDER BEEF WITH ONIONS AND GREEN PEPPERS— BUT NO BEANS—ARE SIMMERED IN A THICK TOMATO SAUCE.

1. Cut beef for stew into ½-inch cubes. Heat oil in 8-quart Dutch oven over high heat, and cook one-third of meat at a time, until browned. With slotted spoon, remove meat cubes to bowl as they brown; set aside.

2. Reserve ½ cup onions; cover and set aside. Add green peppers, garlic, and remaining onions to drippings in Dutch oven; over medium-high heat, cook 10 minutes, stirring occasionally.

3. Return meat to Dutch oven; add tomatoes with their liquid, tomato paste, chili powder, sugar, salt, oregano, black pepper, and 2 cups water; heat to boiling over high heat. Reduce heat to low; cover and simmer 1½ hours or until meat is fork-tender, stirring occasionally.

4. Spoon chili into large bowl. Pass reserved onion to sprinkle over each serving.

EACH SERVING: About 303 calories, 32g protein, 21g carbohydrate, 11g total fat (3g saturated), 85mg cholesterol, 937mg sodium

SWEET CORN PUDDING

INGREDIENTS

- ½ cup (1 stick) unsalted butter
- 1 medium onion, chopped
- 2 cloves garlic, sliced
- 12 ears corn, kernels cut off the cob (about 9 cups), or 3 bags (12 ounces each) frozen corn kernels
- ¼ cup all-purpose flour
- 1 quart heavy cream
- 1 cup cooked grits (from about 6 tablespoons uncooked)
- 3 tablespoons minced canned jalapeño chile peppers
- Salt and ground black pepper, to taste
- 9 large eggs, beaten
- 1 cup (about 4 ounces) shredded white Cheddar

IF IN THE MIDDLE OF WINTER YOU HAPPEN TO HAVE BAGS OF SWEET CORN YOU STASHED IN THE FREEZER OVER THE SUMMER, THIS IS A GREAT WAY TO USE THEM.

1. Preheat oven to 425°F. In heavy-bottomed pot over medium heat, melt butter. Add onion and garlic and cook 3 minutes. Add corn and cook, stirring, 3 to 5 minutes more. Add flour and stir 1 minute, then stir in cream. Continue to stir until mixture comes to a boil, about 15 minutes. Add cooked grits and remove pot from heat. Stir in jalapeños and season with salt and pepper.

2. With handheld immersion blender, puree corn mixture in pot while slowly adding eggs until thoroughly incorporated.

3. Pour mixture into ungreased 9" by 13" baking dish and sprinkle with cheese. Bake until center puffs and top turns golden brown, 25 to 30 minutes.

EACH SERVING: About 556 calories, 13g protein, 29g carbohydrate, 45g total fat (27g saturated), 280mg cholesterol, 166mg sodium

SELF-SERVE HOT-CHOCOLATE BAR

INGREDIENTS

CLASSIC HOT CHOCOLATE

- 7 **cups milk**
- 1 **pound bittersweet chocolate, chopped**
- 1 **cup heavy cream**
- 1 **cup sugar**
- 2 **teaspoons vanilla extract**

WINTER-WHITE HOT CHOCOLATE

- 7 **cups milk**
- 1 **pound white chocolate, chopped**
- 1 **cup heavy cream**
- 2 **teaspoons vanilla extract**
- **Sugar, to taste**

FOR A SWEET AND FESTIVE WINTER PARTY, WHIP UP TWO KINDS OF COCOA: ONE DARK, ONE PALE, BOTH IRRESISTIBLE.

For either variation, bring 7 cups of milk to a simmer in a small pan over low heat, then whisk in the remaining ingredients until smooth.

EACH SERVING (CLASSIC HOT CHOCOLATE): About 618 calories, 13g protein, 63g carbohydrate, 42g total fat (25g saturated), 62mg cholesterol, 104mg sodium

EACH SERVING (WINTER-WHITE HOT CHOCOLATE): About 542 calories, 11g protein, 45g carbohydrate, 36g total fat (22g saturated), 74mg cholesterol, 154mg sodium

HOT CHOCOLATE GARNISHES

SET OUT A SWEET GARNISH STATION: Let guests customize their own drinks with ginger candies, crushed Butterfingers, coconut flakes, mini marshmallows, sliced Kit Kats, and caramel syrup. Chocolate-dipped biscuit sticks and peppermint sticks function as stirrers. And for the adults? Decanters of dark rum and vanilla vodka.

MARDI GRAS BASH

Chicken-&-Andouille Gumbo

Vegetable Muffaletta

Fried-Shrimp Po'Boys

Pecan Pralines

King Cake (store bought)

Sazeracs and Abita to drink

TIMELINE

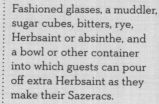

UP TO 1 WEEK IN ADVANCE

• Make the Pecan Pralines and store in airtight containers.

UP TO 3 DAYS IN ADVANCE

• Make the olive salad for the Vegetable Muffaletta and refrigerate.

UP TO 1 DAY IN ADVANCE

• Make the gumbo through step 4; cover and refrigerate.

• Buy, peel, and devein the shrimp for the po'boys and refrigerate, tightly covered.

• Grill the vegetables for the muffaletta and refrigerate.

UP TO 4 HOURS IN ADVANCE

• Assemble the muffaletta, wrap it tightly, and refrigerate.

• Put beer on ice. Cut lemon peels for Sazeracs and refrigerate. Set up a serve-yourself Sazerac station with a large ice bucket and a small bowl to hold lemon peels, Old Fashioned glasses, a muddler, sugar cubes, bitters, rye, Herbsaint or absinthe, and a bowl or other container into which guests can pour off extra Herbsaint as they make their Sazeracs.

• Set out the desserts.

WHEN IT COMES TO LIVENING UP the tail end of a long winter, nothing beats a Mardi Gras party. Order your king cake early (they're available online), retrieve last year's green, gold, and purple bead necklaces from the kids' dress-up bin, put together a jazzy playlist, and lay in plenty of beer because the party could go all night—if you're lucky.

Rather than a sit-down meal, make it a casual serve-yourself affair with DIY po'boys and mixed-to-order Sazeracs. The vegetarian muffaletta can be made in advance to set out on a buffet table alongside a big pot of gumbo and platters of sandwich fixings. These are all dishes that are easily scaled up for a larger crowd. If you'd like, double or triple the po'boy fixings and offer sliced roast beef and debris (drippings and browned bits from the roasting pan) as well as or instead of the last-minute-fried shrimp.

2 HOURS IN ADVANCE

- Prepare for shrimp frying: Put vegetable oil in a large heavy pot for frying the shrimp, put paper towel–lined plate nearby, make egg batter and flour dredge for shrimp.

1 HOUR IN ADVANCE

- Reheat the gumbo and continue with step 5, adding tomatoes and okra.

- Cook white or brown rice on a back burner or in a rice cooker and keep warm.

- Gather and set out toppings for po'boys: shredded lettuce, sliced tomatoes, sauces.

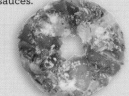

LAST 30 MINUTES

- Warm the po'boy bread in the oven, fry the shrimp.

- Slice the muffaletta.

- Garnish the gumbo.

CHICKEN-&-ANDOUILLE GUMBO

⊰ SERVES 8

INGREDIENTS

- 2½ pounds chicken (2 skinless thighs; 2 large boneless, skinless breast halves)
- ½ teaspoon salt
- ½ cup all-purpose flour
- 1 tablespoon Creole seasoning (such as Tony Chachere's)
- 1 teaspoon garlic powder
- 5 tablespoons canola oil
- 12 ounces andouille sausage links, sliced
- 4 large bell peppers (2 red, 2 green), chopped
- 1 medium onion, chopped
- 6 cups low-sodium chicken broth
- 1 can (15 ounces) diced tomatoes, drained
- 2½ cups sliced frozen okra
- 4 cups cooked rice
- ½ cup chopped fresh parsley

A WARMING STEW FULL OF BRIGHT, CRISP VEGETABLES, LEAN CHICKEN, AND SPICY ANDOUILLE SAUSAGE, THIS GUMBO IS A STICK-TO-YOUR-RIBS DISH THAT'S PERFECT DURING THE COLD WINTER MONTHS.

1. Sprinkle chicken with salt and let sit for 10 minutes. Meanwhile, in large resealable plastic bag, combine ¼ cup flour, Creole seasoning, and garlic powder. In large Dutch oven over medium-high heat, heat 2 tablespoons oil. Add chicken to bag, one piece at a time, and shake to coat. Transfer chicken to pot and cook over medium heat, turning once, until golden brown, about 5 minutes per side.

2. Transfer chicken to paper towel–lined plate and add sausage to pot. Cook until lightly browned, about 3 minutes. Add peppers and onion and cook until slightly softened, 5 to 7 minutes. Transfer sausage-vegetable mixture to bowl and set aside.

3. Wipe pot clean and set over medium-low heat. Add remaining ¼ cup flour and 3 tablespoons oil and stir constantly until a deep-brown roux forms, about 10 minutes. Add sausage-vegetable mixture and stir to combine. Stir in broth, increase heat to medium-high, and bring to a boil. Add chicken, reduce heat to medium-low, and simmer about 40 minutes.

4. Remove chicken from pot and shred into bite-size pieces, discarding thigh bones. Return chicken to pot.

5. Add tomatoes and okra. Simmer until okra is tender, about 10 minutes. Serve over rice. Garnish with parsley.

EACH SERVING: About 538 calories, 45g protein, 42g carbohydrate, 21g total fat (4g saturated), 124mg cholesterol, 1,000mg sodium

VEGETABLE MUFFALETTA

INGREDIENTS

OLIVE SALAD

- ½ cup pitted kalamata olives
- ½ cup pimento-stuffed green olives
- ½ cup fresh flat-leaf parsley leaves
- 1 stalk celery, coarsely chopped
- ½ small onion, coarsely chopped
- 2 tablespoons extra-virgin olive oil
- 2 tablespoons capers
- 1 clove garlic, minced
- 1 teaspoon red wine vinegar

MUFFALETTA

- 1 loaf crusty bread
- 1 (6-ounce) yellow summer squash, cut into ¼-inch-thick lengthwise slices
- 1 (6-ounce) zucchini, cut into ¼-inch-thick lengthwise slices
- 3 roasted red bell peppers
- 3 romaine lettuce leaves
- ¼ pound Provolone cheese, deli-sliced
- 8 ounces fresh mozzarella, cut into thin slices

THE MUFFALETTA IS A SIGNATURE NEW ORLEANS SANDWICH LOADED WITH COLD CUTS. WE'VE STREAMLINED OURS BY SUBSTITUTING WAISTLINE-FRIENDLY VEGETABLES.

1. Prepare olive salad: Combine all ingredients in food processor; pulse until mixture is finely chopped. Pour into a bowl, cover, and marinate in refrigerator.

2. Prepare muffaletta: Slice bread in half horizontally and slightly scoop out some of the insides to accommodate the filling. Spread olive salad over bottom of loaf.

3. Arrange squash and zucchini on grill grate over medium-hot coals. Grill 10 to 12 minutes, until vegetables are crisp-tender, turning once. Layer squash, zucchini, roasted peppers, romaine, Provolone, and mozzarella in hollowed bread, pressing gently after each layer. Repeat layers with remaining vegetables, lettuce, and cheese. Replace bread top and serve immediately or cover with plastic wrap and refrigerate up to 4 hours. Cut into wedges before serving.

EACH SERVING: About 423 calories, 17g protein, 27g carbohydrate, 28g total fat (10g saturated), 46mg cholesterol, 1,053mg sodium

FRIED-SHRIMP PO'BOYS

INGREDIENTS

- 3 cups canola oil, for frying
- 1 large egg
- 1 cup milk
- 2 tablespoons stone-ground mustard (such as Zatarain's Creole Mustard)
- 1 tablespoon yellow mustard
- 2 cups yellow corn flour (such as Bob's Red Mill)
- 4 teaspoons garlic salt
  Salt and ground black pepper
- 2 loaves Italian bread, cut into 8 equal portions
- 2 pounds jumbo shrimp, peeled and deveined
- ½ cup tartar sauce
- 3 cups torn lettuce
- 4 medium tomatoes, sliced
- ½ cup ketchup
  Hot sauce (optional)

A LOUISIANA FAVORITE, THE PO'BOY CAN BE MADE WITH ANY NUMBER OF INGREDIENTS, BUT THE SHRIMP IN THIS VERSION ARE A LIGHT, SWEET CONTRAST TO THE HOT SAUCE AND CRISPY FRIED BREADING.

1. Preheat oven to 375°F. In large cast-iron skillet or heavy pot fitted with candy thermometer, heat oil to 325°F. Meanwhile, in shallow bowl, whisk together egg, milk, 1 cup water, and both mustards; set aside. In medium bowl, combine corn flour and garlic salt. Season with salt and pepper and set aside.

2. Slice bread portions lengthwise and place, crust down, on large baking sheet. Transfer to oven, turn off heat, and warm bread until crisp.

3. Meanwhile, working in batches, dip shrimp in egg batter, then dredge in flour mixture. Fry shrimp in heated oil until they're cooked through and float to surface, 2 to 3 minutes per batch. Transfer to paper towel-lined plate to drain.

4. Spread bottom half of each warmed loaf with 1 tablespoon tartar sauce. Divide lettuce, tomatoes, and shrimp among sandwiches. Drizzle 1 tablespoon ketchup and a few dashes of hot sauce, if desired, over shrimp. Top with remaining bread halves.

EACH SERVING: About 600 calories, 32g protein, 77g carbohydrate, 17g total fat (3g saturated), 209mg cholesterol, 2,177mg sodium

PECAN PRALINES

⊰| MAKES 16

INGREDIENTS

- 5 tablespoons unsalted butter, plus more for parchment
- 1 cup light brown sugar
- 1 cup granulated sugar
- 1 cup melted vanilla-bean ice cream
- 9½ ounces pecans, chopped (2½ cups)
- ½ teaspoon salt

NO MARDI GRAS FÊTE'S MENU WOULD BE COMPLETE WITHOUT SOME SORT OF SWEET TREAT FILLED WITH PECANS, AND THESE PRALINES WILL HIT THE SPOT AFTER A SPICY MEAL.

1. Line two baking sheets with parchment, butter parchment, and set aside. In medium saucepan over medium-low heat, combine both sugars with ice cream, stirring with a clean metal spoon until sugars are dissolved. Using pastry brush dipped in water, brush down sides of pan to prevent sugars from crystallizing.

2. Add 5 tablespoons butter and stir to combine. Fit pan with candy thermometer, increase heat to medium, and let cook until mixture reaches 240°F. Remove from heat and stir in pecans and salt. Stir until slightly opaque, 30 to 60 seconds.

3. Drop praline mixture, by 2 heaping tablespoons, onto prepared baking pans. Let pralines cool until set, about 30 minutes. Serve immediately or store in an airtight container for up to 1 week.

EACH SERVING: About 267 calories, 2g protein, 30g carbohydrate, 17g total fat (4g saturated), 13mg cholesterol, 82mg sodium

PHOTO CREDITS

© Cedric Angeles: 52, 54

© Quentin Bacon: 77, 79, 80, 138

© James Baigrie: 57

© Grant Cornett: 13, 62

© John Dolan: 147

© Miki Duisterhof: 17

Getty Images: © Armstrong Studios 35, © Thomas Barwick 2, © Caiaimage/Paul Bradbury 149 (table), © CSA Images/B&W Archive Collection 36 (chair), © James Carrier 7, © Datacraft Co Ltd 47 (picnic), © Franz Marc Frei 37 (porch), © JGI/Jamie Grill 69 (sprinkler), © Lisa Hubbard 87 (coolers), © Jupiter Images 59 (father & son), 73 (lemonade), © Jessica L 65 (cupcakes), © Michael Paul 97 (table), © Erik Rank 36 (flowers), © Juliette Wade 4, © Barry Winiker 65 (Waldorf)

© Raymond Hom: 18

iStockPhoto: 128 (holly), © Ac Bnphotos, 107, © Casarsa 25 (ham), © CCNUT 40, © ConstantinosZ 209 (cutlery), © Didecs 75 (shells), © Dizzy 69 (peaches), © DNY59 11, 23, 47, 59, 69, 75, 87, 97, 117,129, 141, 149 (paperclip), 212 (mask), © elfirka 128 (ornaments), © Floortje 34, © Gilas 141 (mittens and scarf), © Hidesy 23 (tulips), © Ilbusca 22, 96 (turkey), © Iwka 47 (watermelon), © Ivan-96 10 (horse), © Kcline 58 (cornbread), © Klosfoto 59 (lantern), © Levesquec, 140 (biscotti), © Luissantos84 149 (cake), © Robyn Mac 131 (bagel), © Luigidi Maggio 81, © Mamatea 46 (shuttlecock), © Mecaleha 74 (sailboat), © Molka 146 (hot chocolate), © Popovaphoto 140 (cinnamon), © Ragnarocks 15, © Rouzes 117 (logs), © Saddako 97 (pie), © Schwabel 68 (water balloons), © ScrappinStacy 14, © SpxChrome 86 (football), © Linda Steward 46 (family), © Twoellis 119 (pimentos), © Valentyn Volkov 37 (beer), © Wambi 10 (horseshoe), © Matka Wariatka 116 (cranberries)

© Ray Kachatorian: 72

© John Kernick, 42, 67, 93

© Yunhee Kim: 5, 40

© Kate Mathis: 6, 32, 38, 60, 124

© Maura McEvoy: 135, 144

© Johnny Miller: 108

© Steve Noble: 58 (campfire), 86 (basket), 116 (fire)

© Marcus Nilsson: 100

© Kana Okada: 29, 95, 152, 155

© Andrew Purcell: 120

Shutterstock: © Bienchen-s 11 (mint), © Roberto Castillo 140 (pot), © fotohunter 10, 22, 36, 46, 58, 68, 74, 86, 96, 116, 128, 140, 148 (ribbon), © Jiri Hera 31, © Alen Kadr 69 (napkins), © Onni 148 (profile), © Solveig 68 (ice cream), © Andrej Sv 87 (blanket), © Wiktory 51

© Anson Smart: 123

Stockfood: © Renée Comet 25 (grits), © Colin Cooke 132, © Creative Photo Services 114, © Gallo Images Pty Ltd. 23 (table), © Great Stock! 76, © House & Leisure 75 (table), © Anna Huerta 141 (picnic), © Keller & Keller Photography 21, 41, 90, © Michael Paul 5 (place setting), © Pics On-Line / Probst & Schon 11, © Jan-Peter Westermann 5, 117 (wine), © Tanya Zouev 129 (table)

Studio D: Jeffrey Westbrook, 88

© Christopher Testani: 26

© Mark Thomas: 131 (Strata)

© Johnny Valiant: 70, 105

INDEX

HEARST BOOKS
New York

An Imprint of Sterling Publishing
1166 Avenue of the Americas
New York, NY 10036

Every effort has been made to ensure that all the information in this book is
accurate. However, due to differing conditions, tools, and individual skills, the
publisher cannot be responsible for any injuries, losses, and/or other damages
that may result from the use of the information in this book.

ISBN 978-1-61837-167-6

Distributed in Canada by Sterling Publishing
c/o Canadian Manda Group, 664 Annette Street
Toronto, Ontario, Canada M6S 2C8
Distributed in the United Kingdom by GMC Distribution Services
Castle Place, 166 High Street, Lewes, East Sussex, England BN7 1XU
Distributed in Australia by Capricorn Link (Australia) Pty. Ltd.
P.O. Box 704, Windsor, NSW 2756, Australia

For information about custom editions, special sales, and premium and
corporate purchases, please contact Sterling Special Sales at 800-805-5489
or specialsales@sterlingpublishing.com.

Manufactured in China

2 4 6 8 10 9 7 5 3 1

www.sterlingpublishing.com